hope you enjoy

With love & best wishes

Donia
x

LET YOUR TRUTHS *Set You Free*

A collection of true stories to give hope in your darkest days

DONIA YOUSSEF & JENNY RAYNER

ISBN: 978-1-8380713-2-5

Published by **Tiny Angel Press Ltd.**
Interior Formatting and Design: **Nonon Tech & Design**

Dedication

SARA YOUSSEF,
06.01.1977 - 03.11.2006

LUCY RAYNER
11.10.89 - 05.05.2012

JAMES PETER STEER
28.11.1979 - 13.5.2020

Foreword

by Ruth Sutherland

We can never underestimate the power of stories and lived experiences. Hearing someone else's story can often be the inspiring words we need to hear. This book is a powerful reminder of the importance of human connection, told through the eyes of some brave young people that have found themselves struggling to cope. They bring hope and courage to anyone reading this book.

I first met Jenny and her daughter Becky when we asked Becky to participate in an armchair interview at Council of Samaritans in March 2016. I was then invited to speak at the Lucy Rayner Foundation's "Can Anyone Hear Me?" event in December 2018. As soon as I met the family, I was struck by the great dignity and courage they had. After losing their daughter and sister Lucy to suicide, they showed pure resilience by working with what had happened and turning it into something that will help others. That is an extraordinary thing, and it is utterly inspiring. Jenny has utilized every resource available to the family to be able to bring support to others that may be finding things difficult, including her work with Donia Youssef to write this moving book.

When we find ourselves feeling desperately lost, the most important thing is to be able to acknowledge what has happened. We're often encouraged to get on with things to get through it, but actually being able to talk through your issues and name your feelings is a really powerful and important thing to be able to do. It's accepting how we feel, no matter the emotion and owning our feelings so that we can begin to work through them.

The beautifully written stories in this book remind us that it is possible to recover from terrible things that happen in our lives. When you talk about your feelings and express yourself, you can find the courage and hope to keep going and make the most of your situation, adapting to a new way.

Many of us experience difficult times at one point or another, so it is important to remember that you are not feeling alone in this and that it is only temporary and will pass in time. Talk to a friend or call the Samaritans, because talking about how you feel can help put things into perspective and help you to feel more positive about the future.

Kindness is such an important part of life, so take time for the simple things, like relaxing at home or doing something you enjoy, like reading this book. Look after yourself so you can look after others around you and never underestimate the importance of human connection. If you see someone that you think may need help, start a conversation. You could save their life.

Ruth Sutherland,
Samaritans CEO.

Table of Contents

Introduction

Our world is changing so much around us, and sometimes we can feel overwhelmed by it all. We have no control over outcomes or events that can have a lasting effect on our lives, whether it be at work, in a relationship, affect finance, our physical and mental health, or our living conditions.

This book was put together amidst the Coronavirus Pandemic, where we have both witnessed the fallout and effects it has had on so many people and lives around the world. The unknown can be a scary place for so many people and the worry of what the future looks like for some, who have lost so much during the pandemic.

Given all of these facts, mental health issues in our society, is certainly on the rise as hope for the future is diminishing. We could go into the facts and figures of what that looks like, but that is not what we are concerned about in this introduction. Everyone has mental health, so matter where you are in the world or your life. Let's look at it like; your mental health is a sliding scale, say 0 is - your mental health is very good, and ten is - your mental health is very poor. All of us can sit anywhere on that scale at any given time in our life; all it takes is for a few major life events to happen for your mental health to be affected. Life events could be anything from moving house, loss of a loved one, break up of a relationship, loss of a job, any form of abuse, a near fatal accident where you could have died, surgery gone wrong, trauma giving birth and news of a terminal illness. These are just a few examples, and there are so many things in our lives that can affect your mental health. Put two or three significant life-changing events in a short space of time, and then you have the right conditions for a poor mental health outcome.

How we deal with these life-changing events is the key; we are all made differently, so we all have different levels of resilience. Some people cannot deal with any stress at all and get overwhelmed very quickly, while for others, nothing seems to phase them and can bounce back very quickly. We can sit anywhere between these two polars. There is no right or wrong, good or bad in this, it is just how it is, and we need to understand that everyone is different, and to respect this fact without judgement.

Everyone has a story and the greatest story to be shared is about our personal lives, challenges, struggles, love and joy and hopes for the future. With all the changes happening in the world, we have lost a little hope for your future, and so we wanted to bring out a book that brings some hope in our darkest days especially if you are struggling right now and you are feeling isolated and alone and feel that you cannot reach out just yet. Hopefully, once you have read this book, it will inspire and propel you into action, get you to talk to someone about how you are feeling.

The book 'Let Your Truths Set You Free' is a book that you can pick you up when you feel life is too much and you don't know how you are going to get through the next minute, the next hour, the next day, the next week! The future is a daunting place for you, and we hope by bringing you some true stories of inspiration and resilience to give you hope in those dark days. Stories of real struggle and fight to victory, to come out the other side and go on to achieve love and self-worth. It gives you a feeling of ' if they can do it so can I...' Showing you that out of adversity there is light, and sometimes you need to take it one day at a time, and it all begins and ends with you. You are the master of your ship, and you have the control of steering it in whatever direction you want it to go. You need to know your destination - HOPE.

We want to thank everyone who has taken part in the book, and you are all true inspirations to this world. In telling your stories, we hope that it will help thousands find the right tools to understand themselves and their mental health, to empower, enrich their lives and to realise your full potential whatever that may be.

We have both been through many catastrophic life events, where our mental health has severely suffered, but we are still here pushing forward to share with you all. We choose to live our life of purpose and to give back to the world after all ' Life is what you make it'!

Donia and Jenny x

Alex

My name is Alex, I'm 28, and I was formally diagnosed with depression almost four years ago. It was an incredibly trying and uncertain period of my life, and at the time, I wasn't sure the feelings I was experiencing would ever come to an end. Thankfully with medical aid and a network of

support, I was able to overcome the overwhelming feeling of darkness, enabling me to be sat here in the present day and reflect on my mental health journey.

Growing up, I had a great childhood and was lucky to be raised surrounded by family in a beautiful part of Surrey. On the whole, I enjoyed school very much and spent all my spare time either playing outside on my bike or dancing, with lessons and competitions being a massive part of my life. They helped to build confidence, friendships with other children of all ages and developed resilience to criticism, which I've always believed is such a valuable life lesson. Although outgoing, I would say that I was definitely an anxious child. Not in the sense of being shy and being scared to try new things, but always fearful of the future and what might happen. There would be no problem with me making friends with a new group or putting my hand up in class to answer a question, but there was always an undercurrent of perhaps not feeling good enough, not looking the part, or feeling or looking silly. I couldn't bare the thought of bending the rules and being caught for anything. If I was out with one of my older sisters and they parked on a double yellow line and ran into a shop for 2 minutes, I would be sent into a frenzy of worry that we'd get a parking ticket. These feelings never actually prevented me from doing anything, I would always try, but my initial reaction was always 'I can't do it', to whatever the task in hand was. It's difficult to pinpoint exactly when and why these feelings were triggered, but there were general periods when things would be noticeably worse. It was always an ongoing joke about how I was a hypochondriac, even at 7 I would be confiding to my dance teacher that I felt sick, I had a pain in my arm and that I thought it was going to lead to a heart attack. Even though this was probably only about 20 years ago, I'm pretty sure in this present day, my symptoms and mindset would be picked up as childhood anxiety. Still, back then there was not so much of a focus on mental health, especially in children.

The early years of secondary school were much the same. Of course, there were issues with teasing, boys saying mean things about my appearance, not being in the 'in' crowd and getting called names etc., but I feel that most children and teenagers go through this at some point in their school life. I'm thankful that I was a strong character and was able to experience this without being deeply affected too much. Of course, it would have been nice to be popular, to be admired or to be the fashion icon of the year on mufti day, but if I knew then what I knew now I would be much happier with my social status and the fact that I was not only able to stick up for myself but also for other people who were having a tough time and perhaps weren't so resilient. Kindness will always overpower popularity, and this is something I hope to instil in my future children one day. It was around year ten that all our lessons were mixed around and I began to make friends with the group I am still friends with now. It's probably around this time that I would notice a significant difference in my mood. We would laugh until we cried at school and I specifically remember saying at the time 'Oh no, I'm so annoyed this has happened because I know within an hour my mood will hit rock bottom'. It was like clockwork. I could go from hysteria to completely miserable, and it was mostly always kicked off by a previous laughing fit. Now who knows, this could have just been a case of teenage hormones. But now having been diagnosed with a mental health issue, it seems significant that I can pinpoint specific times that I was able to foresee a dark mood descending before it hit. Is this something I should have taken more notice of?

My later teens and into young adult life were probably where my childhood worries would have been a lot more justified. Both my parents suffered ill health, and when I was 16, my mum underwent treatment for stage 3 bowel cancer. Then when I was 17, my dad suffered a catastrophic stroke, leaving him permanently immobilized. As you can imagine, both these scenarios have been significantly life changing, with my mum being continuously unwell and left somewhat weaker since over-coming her illness and my dad being left unable to walk and needing care for everyday living. As with anything, at the time it was very much business as usual for me, and perhaps quite surprisingly, considering my anxious childhood nature, I was able to continue with college, exams etc. and just try to keep my head down and overcome my sadness, fear and anxiety of what the future might hold. Of course, it was an incredibly worrying time and looking back I think subconsciously I didn't fully appreciate the effect it had on my teenage self, with the suppressed feelings coming out in later life.

I carried on and went to university in Twickenham, staying in halls of residence and then a flat for the final two years. I wanted to be close by so I could come home every weekend. The general stresses of uni life ticked along, but it was in my third year when I succumbed to the way I was feeling not being normal. It was as if everything just became too much, and the way I had been balancing my emotions and responsibilities so far just didn't work for me anymore. I couldn't focus on my work, even though I was undoubtedly in the most crucial year of my studies. It was almost like the feeling of not being able to sleep when you know you need it for the day that's in store tomorrow. No matter what you try, nothing is working, and all you keep doing is counting down the time you have left to make a difference. Instead of bringing the problem home, I decided to consult with a university counsellor, not knowing what to say or how to act because I couldn't single out one particular issue that was making me feel this way. If I'm honest, I can't remember any significant enlightenment coming out of those sessions, if anything it was an hour a week to sit in peace and quiet without the guilt of not doing any work. Perhaps it helped, as I made it through to graduating.

It was right at the end of university, that I was first diagnosed with an underactive thyroid. It was a surprise as the reason for going to the doctor in the first place was for a suspected overactive thyroid, an issue that ran in the family. However, it turned out that my whole body was on the go slow. The symptoms that are associated with the condition (weight gain, depression, low mood, etc.) were not fully explained at the time; I was just relieved that my ongoing sleepiness was explained! After being medicated and going for a checkup around two years later, it transpired that signs had shown up in blood tests years earlier in my first year of university when I'd had glandular fever, but nobody had acted on it or told me. Who knows, could this have been bubbling away even before this, during school years and could it have been the reason for my unpredictable moods?

And so we fast forward to diagnosis. A continuous period of low mood, no motivation and uncertainty about my own life and what I should be doing led me to this point. It's all a bit hazy, but the start was a referral from the doctor for a telephone assessment. This took place in a coffee shop on my lunch hour and even this at the time felt too monumental to handle. The series of questions asked led me to tears as the man on the phone asked 'and what do you see for your future' and my response was 'nothing, I just see grey'. I knew I didn't want to die. That was never a question. I just wanted to know I wouldn't be consumed by this mindset forever. I didn't want to live this way with this outlook anymore, and so I accepted help. Firstly I was prescribed a 6-week course of CBT therapy. This in itself was a massive challenge to juggle along with working a full-time job in a new role that I was uncertain of anyway. I would have to drive half an hour to start the therapy for 8 am and then go straight on to work afterwards. The whole experience was just too much. I continued to be down and have a lack of motivation, with my behaviour upsetting those around me. I just was not myself. The process didn't work for me, and in the last session, the therapist said to me, my mind was not in the right state to have been undergoing this type of therapy.

She said it would have been much more effective if I'd been medicated first. This hadn't even been offered or discussed yet, so back to the doctors it was.

I sat with my doctor for the third time and broke down. Nothing had yet worked, and all I wanted was a magic wand to fix everything. I had never been against taking medication at all; it had just not however been discussed as an option. Although this time was different; I was prescribed 20mg of Citalopram and was signed off work. The idea was just to take a step back and relieve myself of at least one stress, giving myself space to focus on my mind and feeling better while allowing the medication to kick in. Of course, all sounded great, but along with this time off came uncertainty. What would I fill my day with other than my own thoughts if I had no focus? How would I explain to people why I was off sick? For exactly how long would this be for? My thoughts whirred, and from what I can remember, I spent a lot of the time lying down without even the energy to clear the bed before I got into it. There was no magic wand. This was going to be a long process, and this was only the start, but I could not see the wood for the trees, and I needed to start somewhere.

But of course, we carry on. Eventually, the fog began to clear as the medication kicked in, and my thoughts and feelings began to be easier to process. I can't pinpoint the actual time I could hand on heart say I felt entirely better because I don't think it ever happened. I think once a mental health issue has touched you; it will always be in the back of your mind, knowing your brain can behave that way. Life moves along, and situations change, but even when you feel better and happy, there is always the fear of 'what if it happens again'. But then again, at least once you have got through it once there is hope should it happen again. Going back to normal life was a struggle, but I am pleased in just this short amount of time since this happened to me that attitudes and awareness of mental health issues have changed for the better, although there is still a long way to go.

So that's the story! Although it may be four years since an official diagnosis, it's clear to see when it's written in black and white that there may have been issues bubbling away before everything came to a head. To this day I still take the same medication, and I'm hoping one day in the near future, I have the courage to be weaned off them, but if I can't, then that's fine too. I see them as nothing more than a substitute for a chemical my body doesn't produce, much like me taking thyroxine for my underactive thyroid.

From my experience, all I can hope for is that the buzz around mental health continues to grow. If I'm completely honest, I think there will always be a hint of stigma around mental health issues, and this will always come from people that have no experience of what it's like to either have them themselves or be close to somebody who does. It's all about understanding, and humans will always be wary of something they don't fully understand. Nobody can walk in somebody else's shoes, but the more we can educate, the smaller this stigma will become. And that is my vision for the future!

Charley

I don't think I can tell you the exact point in time when it all started to go pear-shaped. I just know from my teens I wasn't happy, and I struggled to process emotions appropriately.

I had two significant traumatic events that seem to be the catalyst that kicked it all off into overdrive. When I was thirteen, and I had a perforated appendix and salmonella food poisoning which resulted in a two-week hospital stay, an operation and some horrific details I won't gross you out with. I almost died, and it was pretty savage. Then at fourteen, eighteen months later, I was in a nasty car accident in which, again, I was fortunate to walk away from.

Before these two events, my childhood was good. No significant physical or emotional trauma, my parents were loving and supportive, and there was always food in the fridge and a roof over our heads. Looking back now, however, I didn't like to be different, and I felt like I had to be a certain way to be accepted. I did not feel like I could be myself and so I would lie and exaggerate about big things and silly little stuff. I always wanted to be the centre of attention for my talents, but I would also like to get lost in my own little world, and I would sit and read for hours at a time. The long and the short of it, I never really felt comfortable in my own skin, and I felt I needed and wanted to be something I wasn't.

It was assumed initially that my mental health was as a result of the accident, and it did spark off a massive change in my personality but to be honest, I was already playing up and getting into trouble. For example, the night of the accident, I was grounded, and I wasn't allowed out. That didn't matter to me though; I called my friends on the sly to come and pick me up. When they were outside, I ran out of the house, jumped into the car, but my mum chased me, and as we drove away, she shouted stop and banged both of her hands on the bonnet. I told my friends to keep going and just drive. It was on the way back to my house, a few hours later, that the accident occurred. Karma bit me in the arse that night!

It had gotten dark and started to rain heavily while I was out. The visibility was poor, especially on the back lanes, and my friend was driving too fast. He mistook how sharp a corner was, and the car began to slide. I don't remember anything past that point up until I was sitting on the side of the road, surrounded by emergency services' crew and covered in blood. I have since been told the vehicle slid until it hit the bank, rolled and ended up in a ditch, almost upside down, leaning its roof on a fence. I was knocked out for a few minutes and then began screaming. I managed to climb out of the car, and a member of the public had stopped and called 999. He let me use his phone to ring my parents as I was screaming hysterically. My dad turned up pretty quick as it was about a mile down the road from home. Then, there I was, sitting on the side of the road, head in my hands, amidst the chaos, in the eye of the storm. It was like being in a film, everything was in slow motion and the noise was distant like I was underwater. I looked to my left to see one of my pals seated next to me wearing an oxygen mask; the driver was standing to the left of him, not a scratch on him. There were police, paramedics and firefighters everywhere. I looked behind me to see fire crew attempting to cut my other mate out of the car; he had been sitting next to me in the back. I hadn't had my seatbelt on when we crashed, I landed on him, and he broke his arm badly, in four places. I turned back to see my dad standing in front of me, looking slightly pale but with a face like thunder. I put my head in my hands and thought to myself, "I am in proper trouble here". That was when I noticed the blood, my blood. It was everywhere, all over my hands and dripping onto my new Nike hoodie. The right side of my face was pouring with claret.

I remember arguing with the ambulance crew about cutting my hoodie off of me in case I had a neck injury, it was ruined from all the blood, but I was adamant they weren't cutting it, they did anyway. I remember kicking off because I had lost my phone, my new Nokia 3310 and I remember being in A&E and going into shock. They managed to stop the bleeding, and I had scans and other tests, but, luckily, I escaped without any broken bones or internal injuries. I woke up the next day in a children's ward with this massive bandage stuck to the side of my face. Covered in blood, scrapes, cuts, bruises and mud and aching in places I didn't know it was possible to ache. I remember pulling a stick out of my tangled, blood-matted, long, brown hair and noticing the dirt in my nails and all over my hands and arms and the dried blood. My blood! I looked like an extra from a zombie movie.

I had to have surgery a few days later in a specialist plastic surgery unit to put my face back together. I looked a right sight, one side of my face completely normal, the other, swollen, black and blue with the best shiner I've ever had or seen since. A three-hour operation and eighty stitches later I was sent home, but I had to keep going back as an outpatient for another two years. They did a fantastic job; the scars are hardly visible today. My body healed, but my mind didn't, and from there, my ability to manage everyday life began to unravel.

We know now that I developed borderline personality disorder which is also known as an emotionally unstable personality disorder. This condition is as a result of trauma in childhood, whether that be physical or mental and is the inability to regulate emotions. Other traits include impulsive, dangerous, self-harming behaviours, suicidal thoughts and addiction. However, this was only diagnosed around three years ago, previous to this; I was unaware that the way I felt and acted was not healthy. I was so lost, and in so much pain, I didn't know what to do with myself, and I was furious at the world. I could not cope with everyday life and fought so hard not to lose myself. I turned to chasing oblivion and running as hard and as fast as I possibly could from reality.

From the age of fourteen to twenty-nine, the only way I got through life was to self-medicate. I had begun smoking weed and drinking down the park with my pals from the age of about twelve. After the accident, my drug use escalated quickly, and it soon became the thing my life revolved around. I couldn't stay high all the time though and when it was time to come down, boy, did I come down! I considered suicide every day, and I regularly self-harmed.

One night, my family and I were in a restaurant out for my dad's birthday. I had rolled my sleeves up without thinking and had the word HELP carved into my arm. My mum saw it and the next day dragged me down the doctors kicking and screaming. I was referred to the Child and Adolescent Mental Health Services, and family therapy began. By this point, I was furious, disruptive, disobedient and generally horrible to be around. My violent outbursts had already started at home, and I had little respect for anyone, including myself. The therapy didn't last long; I think I only had a few one-on-one sessions and a couple of family therapy sessions. I can't really remember what was discussed except my mum being adamant that my behaviour was as a result of the accident, she said it was as if I had changed personalities overnight. I disagreed, I just thought I hated my parents and they were ruining my fun, aka taking drugs.

One session I do remember resulted in mum, dad and I all standing up screaming at each other while my ten-year-old sister, sat with her hands over her ears, crying and shouting at us to stop. That was literally what life was like for all of us in a moment. It is only now, at thirty-two do I realise the impact my behaviour had on all of us. Am I ashamed and regretful? Of course, I am, my family did not deserve what I put them through. However, I feel more sadness that no one was there to help us. Shortly after that session, I did not return to therapy, even though my poor mum was convinced my personality had changed. My EUPD was not picked up, and I fell through the cracks in the system, and I ended up using drugs again! My drug use changed and adapted as I got older, becoming more socially acceptable and less about losing control and more about giving me confidence and the ability to be ok in myself. The drugs changed, where I used changed, the way I used changed, the people I used with changed, but the reason I used, did not.

Fast forward to 2016, at twenty-nine years old, I had managed to escape from an abusive relationship. My ex-boyfriend had put me through mental, physical, financial and emotional hell for four years. Thankfully and finally the police were called one night and with it became the beginning of the end of the abuse. I moved back to London to get away from my ex, and the police referred me for domestic violence counselling. While having counselling for the trauma, my therapist suggested that I attend a twelve-step meeting for drug addiction. That night I walked into my first meeting. I can't remember what was shared, but I remember hearing a message of hope, and I identified with the pain and feelings the other addicts were talking about. I remember someone getting up at the end of the meeting and getting a year clean time keyring and wondering how the hell they did it.

A year felt so far away; I couldn't go a day without using some substance to avoid reality. I also remember hearing about how alcohol is a drug and thinking; 'I've come here to stop taking drugs, no one said anything about the booze!' I did not know how on god's green earth I was going to stop drinking. I kept thinking of all the weddings, birthdays, Christmases and holidays and knowing I would not be able to get through it without a drink. I came into recovery, thinking I had a drug problem. I now know I have a me problem! I will use whatever I can to change the way I feel, and it is not about the substance I am using. I have addictions to drugs, alcohol, food and sex, and I am co-dependent. Those are the obvious issues, but they are just symptoms of a bigger problem, me!

I managed to stay clean for ten days after that first meeting then I relapsed on alcohol. I went to a meeting the following day, owned my shit, and since then, 22nd March 2017, I have been clean from drugs and alcohol. It has not been easy by any stretch of the imagination, but it is by far, the best thing I have ever done for myself, my life and the people I love and care about.

It wasn't until I stopped using that it became apparent how much of an addict I really was. I struggled every day to sit with myself, the pain and thoughts in my head. All I wanted to do was suppress it and find oblivion. It also became apparent how mentally ill I really was. The first ninety days were tough, I just existed, and the people around me had to watch as I fell into a deeper and deeper darkness.

I was so lost, and it felt never-ending. I cannot allow myself ever to go back to that state of mind. To this day, it frightens the hell out of me, and I honestly do not know how I got through it alive. At the time, I was in so much emotional pain and to deal with the turmoil I was in, I disassociated. I stopped eating and looking after myself, and I smoked cigarettes almost continuously, the only reason I would leave my room.

I was lucky enough to be surrounded by people who cared about me and could see I was not myself. My two closest friends from uni looked after me and kept an eye on me. Emily used to come over and cook me food, and she wouldn't let me go anywhere until I'd eaten and would literally sit and watch me eat. My housemate Lizzie would put me in and out of the bath and used to cuddle me when I couldn't stop crying. Rey, Lizzie's boyfriend, would walk me to the train station, and one of my tutors would have to come and meet me at London Bridge to walk me to uni.

I considered suicide every day. An incident within my family a few years previously enabled me to see what it would be like to be on the other side of a suicide attempt. It stopped me attempting suicide for four months, but then it got to a point where I couldn't hold on anymore.

I spectacularly failed a clinical exam, potentially endangering a patient and being graded a G, meaning unfit for practice. This was very out of character for me and well below my usual standard. My clinical work was where I shone in my studies. I was so out of it though, I can't even really remember it, and when the results came in, my tutor pulled me into her office. She took one look at me, knew straight away there was something severely wrong and took me directly to A&E, herself. I went with a packed bag, expecting to be sectioned as I had a letter from my GP requesting this action immediately for my own safety. However, the guy doing the psych assessment didn't think I was ill enough to be warranted a hospital stay, and I was sent home and told to wait for a referral back to the community mental health team, a six-week wait. Once again, my tutor stepped in and called the hospital the next day and arranged for me to go into the crisis center, they also arranged a meeting with my parents.

I should probably mention, during this time, I was in my final year of a four year Masters degree in Osteopathy. My dissertation was due, my final exams were upon me, and I was struggling to deal with the pressure of uni, my mental health, getting clean and the trauma from the domestic violence. With my tutors' support, I was able to tell my parents what was going on, and we all came up with a plan for my studies. I deferred my course for a year to enable me to concentrate on getting well and staying clean. In actual fact, it would take me an extra two years to be stable enough to be able to complete my degree.

The alleviation of pressure surrounding uni meant I took a step back from the suicidal ledge I was precariously perched on, and I didn't need to be admitted into the crisis centre. I did, however, have to attend every day, and it was there that I was diagnosed with my mental health conditions, depression, anxiety, borderline personality disorder and post-traumatic stress disorder. I was put on antidepressants, and a plan was put together for my future care and treatment.

From there it has been a long, winding road back to any kind of normality, one that I am still walking. On being discharged from the crisis centre, I was referred to the community mental health team. From there, to the complex needs team and an almost two-year wait to get the recommended therapy I needed. That is a very brief, straightforward description of the process. In reality, it was like trudging through treacle. I had to battle with GPs, psychiatrists and support workers to get where I needed to be. At times I've been taken off waiting lists by one practitioner, only to be put back on by another, delaying the process even further. It's been painful and long-winded and at times never-ending but I am where I need to be now.

I am still on medication, and it took two years for them to stabilise me. I am currently on a treatment programme specifically for people who suffer from issues regulating emotions which consisted of a ten-week course last year on mentalisation and how to use it in everyday life and in therapy. Two months ago, I began an eighteen-month programme of one-to-one counselling and group therapy every week. I realise how lucky I am to be under the care of the complex needs team. It is not available in many areas, and the waiting list is far too long. I managed to hold on until the therapy started but its been touch and go at times.

The therapy is going ok; it is bringing up a lot of feelings and pain, something that I don't particularly like. One saying you hear in recovery is 'the good thing about being clean is you get your feelings back, the bad thing about being clean is you get your feelings back'. Ain't that the truth! I do not do well with feelings. I've grown up handling emotions in a different way to everybody else. I am a pro at pushing stuff down and putting on a mask, pretending I am ok and portraying to the world, and to myself, strength and stability when I am actually dying inside.

Sometimes, I don't know why I am feeling the way I am. I have just had to get to grips with the unknown and be ok with it. I just, at that moment in time, have to sit in pain and try not to change it, because that is what I am an expert in, changing the way I feel. Whether it be with drugs, alcohol, food, sex or box sets, if I can try and alter or stop my feelings of discomfort, I will.

It is a work in progress, not every day is fantastic, but I have support today, and I have tools which allow me to climb out of the dark holes I can find myself in.

The majority of the time I am fine, but sometimes things can get on top, and I feel like I need the world to stop so I can get off. Getting off the booze and drugs may have been good for me, but that doesn't mean it's been easy. I've known what it means to be lonely since I got clean, I can be in a room full of people, friends even, and feel so alone. I lost my motivation for life since getting clean. It has come back in drips and drabs, but there are still elements of my life that have not returned. I love my food, eating, watching and planning meals, but my ability and motivation to cook has gone out the window. This applies to my fitness too. I used to run, it would help with my anxiety and clear my head, but that stopped in the first few months of recovery.

I trained in musical theatre all through my childhood; it was my chosen profession from an early age. I was one of those annoying people who was constantly dancing and singing without even realising. Music was my life. I sang in the shower, in the car, when I was cooking, when I was sad and when I was happy. I do not know when, but it stopped.

These are the things I am working on. I am actively looking to start singing and piano lessons again soon and I went to a dance fitness class yesterday for the first time in a long while. It is all a work in progress. Today may not be perfect, and I may not complete the tasks I need too, but that's ok. It's progression, not perfection and every day I step a little bit further away from the past and the pain and into a future filled with self-worth, stability and love. To quote Ewan McGregor from the film Moulin Rouge, 'all you need is love' and don't I appreciate and fully understand that today. Life isn't about the materialistic; it's about filling your world with love and kindness and leaving a mark that is to be admired. Karma will give you what you deserve if all you do is take and hurt people along the way.

A phrase I heard recently which I love and represents keeping it in the moment is "If you keep one foot in the past and one foot in the present, you'll piss all over today". That's anxiety right there. If you keep worrying about what's happened and what may or may not happen, you miss out on today.

If something is stressing me out today, I have a chat with myself and then leave it up to the universe. If it's meant to be, it will be. I write a list every morning of ten things I am grateful for, and I meditate for ten minutes. As long as I look after myself, don't harm anyone and try and be the best version of myself for me and the rest of the world, then it has been a good day. If I keep myself present and know that feelings pass, I can stay clean, just for today because today is all we have. Tomorrow isn't promised so don't waste a second of it worrying about things you cannot control or change.

I want to say thank you to my family, friends and the Lucy Rayner Foundation for never giving up on me even when I had given up on myself. I will leave you with two prayers I say to myself every day, sometimes repeatedly. Especially in traffic!

Let my soul be at peace, my spirit free, and my mind untroubled and clean.

Grant me the serenity to accept the things I cannot change, the courage to change the things I can, and the wisdom to know the difference.

You, and nobody else, are in charge of your destiny. Things can get better, and things do get better. Don't give up before the miracle arrives.

Charley xxxx

Chenelle

From surviving to thriving
A story of post-traumatic growth after childhood sexual abuse

BACKGROUND ABOUT ME AND MY STORY

I have always had an unparalleled desire to share my story; to share my truth. It is only now that I feel brave enough, or perhaps I mean safe enough, to open up and share my experiences. I hope that those of you reading this, who have been through similar trauma, gain some comfort from the words written in these pages. I will honestly share my journey, and I hope that you will feel some solidarity in battling the stigma and the shame bestowed on us. We should feel no shame – we should be able to shout out to the winds what we have been through, with pride at fighting back the stigma that allows these horrendous acts to continue. I want to tell you that I see you, that you're not alone, and that what happened to you, and the daily battles you have faced as a result are not your fault. So, here it goes.

My grandad sexually abused me. My first memory is when I was just aged 3, and the abuse continued until I was 9, when he died. I was naive about his actions and the immorality of them. I had no idea that what was happening was wrong because it was made to feel normal. I recall moments of feeling afraid, the glimpses of his expression that made me feel uneasy and my awkward giggles, but ultimately, at the time, it was a part of my day to day life, and it was the only thing I knew.

I remember the day that I realised what had happened. I was 11 years old, and I was in the car with my mum. I was due to stay over my aunt's house, and my family were all quite concerned about how trustworthy her boyfriend was. My mum talked me through keeping myself safe, and it just clicked. That night I remember feeling afraid, and the next day at school I couldn't hold it in, so I told a friend. The experience of disclosure for me was awful. My friend confided in a work experience student, who in turn told my teacher. This all happened while I was in the playground, and I remember feeling sheer terror at the consequences of having told someone. My teacher at the time was male, and when we went back into the classroom, he asked to have a word with me. He took me to the disabled toilet, and once inside, asked me if I was telling the truth. I remember having the realisation then that people may not believe me, and I almost immediately started to question my own memories – "Was I making it all up? Did it actually happen?". My teacher took me to the head teacher's office, something that usually only happened when you'd been naughty. I had to wait with her for my mum to turn up, but my mum wasn't allowed in until a social worker could observe us. I was made to tell my mum myself, in the presence of the headteacher and social worker, despite not feeling able to. I had to leave school that day and Mum took me out and bought me something nice, that's my mum's way of showing love.

After the disclosure, my family did the best they could to sweep everything under the carpet. It was too painful for them, and they didn't know how to handle it. I didn't realise at the time, but they had asked for support, and social services had said: "there's nothing we can do, the perpetrator is dead, and so we are closing the case". It was only years later, while formulating my experiences in therapy, that I realised the gravity of what happened to me, and that the shame and guilt I felt for struggling with my own mental health came from the unconscious message of those who were supposed to protect me. My family also wanted to "protect" other people – my nan who was married to him and was old and frail, my Nanna who would "die of the pain", me...because apparently, people would use it against me for the rest of my life. These were the messages I received about the danger of honesty. So, of course, I felt that I must stay quiet, not show the inner turmoil that was beginning to suffocate me. I also learnt, through all the messages I had received, that it was not a big deal, I thought I must have been making a fuss, and it wasn't that bad. It made me feel guilty for feeling any emotions at all about it.

When my nan died, soon after, my dad confided in my aunt as he wanted to swap his dad's wedding ring for his mums. At this point, it came out that my aunt had also been abused. I remember at the time feeling, not anger, like my mum, but relief that my memories must be reliable. That I wasn't "crazy" or "a liar", and that the blanks in my memory, and the disorganised way they would replay, wasn't because I was delusional. I've since learnt that traumatic memories encode like that, and what I experienced was completely normal. I suffered traumatic amnesia for some of the memories, as a protective mechanism. However, I was also laden with guilt that I felt reassurance that I wasn't alone. Surely, that made me a bad person? To feel comfort in another person's suffering.

I struggled immensely with my emotions throughout my adolescence, but I learned to wear a mask. I had a superpower at the time, and that was my academic ability. I put everything into my schoolwork, so everyone thought I was just fine. I went to a grammar school, and I got excellent grades. At the same time, I used to go home and cry myself to sleep every night. I would draw in a diary and grapple with feeling strong emotions of love and hate simultaneously, with no understanding of that possibility. Complicated feelings are hard for adults to navigate, and I was still a child. I also started self-harming not long after the disclosure. I would self-harm in the evenings, and it would provide me with an outlet from the emotional pain I felt, at least temporarily. This grew into self-punishment once my effort at repressing my pain led to it seeping out through "negative" behaviours. I remember thinking "What is wrong with me? I must be inherently bad", and genuinely believe this. I know now that harming myself only contributed to a cycle of self-abuse, while not resolving any of the deeper causes of my pain. It brings me grief to look back at my younger self, and all she went through, all alone.

I tried to remedy my feelings of worthlessness and unresolved pain through seeking love. Unfortunately, I conflated love with sex, and therefore from the age of 13, I sought affection in all the wrong places. I got into a 6-month abusive relationship with a 16-year-old, who was controlling and aggressive. I then became more and more promiscuous, because I thought that was how to express love, and how I would, in turn, feel loveable one day. Unfortunately, the void was never filled, and my behaviour led to further suffering due to my family expressing shame and anger, my peers' slut-shaming me, and the boys I was trying to receive love from seeing me as an 'easy ride'.

On top of that, I was deeply ashamed of myself and how worthless I was. Each time someone slept with me and then ignored my calls or told their friends I was a whore and shamed me, or told me I was "too much", I would see it as more and more evidence that I was bad and unworthy. I went through a lot of pain and suffering, and it ultimately strengthened my deeply held beliefs of being unlovable, shameful, bad. At the same time, as all of this, my own home life began to become more and more unstable.

As well as the abuse I experienced as a child; I also grew up as a child of a mother with mental health problems. My mum has severe obsessive-compulsive disorder. Throughout my childhood, my mum would commit hours to cleaning the house, and as I got older, this got progressively worse. We weren't allowed anyone else around the house, as they might move things out of order, or create a mess, upsetting the perfection of the prior hours of ritualising. This also led to a severe amount of anxiety for us all. We lived in fear of making a mess by accident or doing something that would trigger mum's anxiety. We lived dictated by routine, and as we got a bit older (and therefore were deemed to be able to alter our behaviour), we spent less and less time as a family.

Even before my disclosure, mum became so transfixed with keeping the living room perfect, that we weren't allowed to step foot in it. I remember dreaming of all watching the TV together or playing games and laughing. I remember feeling like my house didn't feel like a home and feeling like an unwelcome visitor. As a result of this, I spent most of my time in my bedroom. While younger, I'd go in my brother's room, and we'd watch TV together. Sometimes dad would come up and watch TV with us, but this often resulted in an argument between my mum and dad because he would be drinking and say something about mum. Mum would be listening, and then, later, when I was tucked up in bed, I would lay awake scared while they shouted at each other. As we got older, my brother started going out with his friends and spent as little time in the house as possible. This left me feeling alone, and I'd try and pass my time escaping my world through schoolwork and reading. It became an addiction to escape my pain and loneliness.

After my disclosure things got worse, my mum and dad would argue relentlessly. I don't remember a night that they didn't. I would lay in bed, not only afraid of my own emotions but fearful of the chaos downstairs. I distinctly remember the hatred in my mum's voice, when she would say "you look just like him. I see you walking down the garden, and I feel sick, I can't bear it". I remember feeling ashamed that I'd caused their relationship to be even worse. I took responsibility for their hatred for each other, and I beat myself up even more about it. After all, in my mind, I deserved it. The tension in the home caused my dad to be extremely explosive too. I think he struggled to cope with my mum's emotions, and he would occasionally, as a result, and after drinking excessively, take it out on my brother or me. When I would "misbehave" he would get extremely aggressive. This resulted in physical abuse too. At one point, he was so angry at me; he pulled me across the room by my hair and threatened to burn my face with my straighteners. He was spitting, and his tone was venomous. I was terrified. At other times, he would hit me. I remember the most hurtful act was when he slapped me straight across my face. I don't know why it was something to do with pride. He used to come in later, crying, and say how sorry he was. My perception was only that that was normal. After all, abuse was my reality.

As I got older, I spent more and more time in my room. This was especially so on a Friday or Saturday night when I'd feel frustrated because nobody would be able to go out. I found some neighbours who would all sit in the living room, and we'd sing karaoke and drink tea. I remember thinking that I wished my home was like that.

When I was 16, I met someone who deeply intrigued me. He had a fascinating aura, a curious and intelligent mind, and would capture the attention of anyone around him. I later learned that his name was Oscar and that he had been sexually abused as a child too. Knowing this and developing such admiration for how open and honest he was about it, led me to want to get to know him further. This led to us having an incredibly intense relationship. I fell deeply for him, and in Oscar, I finally found someone who understood me. Unfortunately, despite our care for each other, we were a couple of kids with deep wounds. Oscar had PTSD, and he was dependent on drugs and alcohol. He was regularly suicidal, self-harmed and dealt with drugs to make a living. I had a naïve optimism where I believed I would save him through love. What happened instead, was that we became emotionally entangled in a toxic play of desperation and emotional pain. Oscar was unable to love me, and it further deepened my belief that I was unlovable. This sent me spiralling down a path of drug-taking and, ultimately, deep depression.

This was the point in my journey where I realised, I wouldn't be able to get through this on my own. So, bravely, I booked a GP appointment for myself. I went there alone with a note I had written in a dark moment, expressing my desire to hurt myself and end my life. The GP I saw didn't make eye contact with me throughout the consultation, despite me sobbing about how low I felt. She was a matter of fact and sent me away with a leaflet for paid counselling sessions, as I did not meet the criteria for CAMHS support. I was devastated and completely disillusioned as a result of this. I remember the last flame of hope being quickly diminished at that moment. It was almost like a light went out.

I struggled on for a couple of weeks! Then one night, while staying with Oscar, I felt utterly overwhelmed. I asked Oscar to stay with me, but he was drunk and was unable to be emotionally available. He left the room, and at that moment, I felt like nobody would ever care about me, and I'd be better off dead. It was then that I went into the bathroom and took a load of pills. The tablets were large and circular, and I couldn't swallow them. So, I stood there, in desperate tears, breaking each tablet in half. They were hard to break, and I remember feeling rage...I wanted this over quickly! I suddenly became distressed and angry at myself and threw the rest of the tablets at the mirror before falling to the floor and weeping. I rocked myself and hugged my knees, like a mother trying to comfort her child. The darkness I felt at that moment was so terrifying. Even as I write now, I feel breathless. After this, I took myself back to bed and told Oscar, who said I'll be fine and to go to sleep. I did fall asleep. The next morning, I luckily awoke, and the gravity of the situation hit me. I was being sick constantly and felt extremely weak. We called an ambulance, and I was taken to the hospital. The paramedics were unkind and showed no empathy at all. It was another moment in my life where I felt unworthy of the presence of the professionals who were supposed to keep me safe.

In the hospital, it all felt very alarming, and I was medicated to counteract the effects of the drugs. They saved my life. It was at this point that I had an assessment with a psychologist. He was kind and warm. I spoke to him about my experiences, and he built up a flicker of hope in me. I remember him saying "this is the reason I do my job, to help people like you. I know you will work hard in therapy and you want the support." I remember asking him if he'd be my therapist, as he showed compassion I had never received before, but he worked in a different trust to my local one. I was fast-tracked for CAMHS support, and I had my first appointment the next day. That was the start of the long road I have walked to healing.

I worked hard in my CAMHS therapy and received treatment for six months. I learnt Cognitive Behavioural Therapy techniques, and I gradually started to realise that I was not unlovable nor unworthy. I became more functional, and I began to see my self-worth. Unfortunately, I turned 18, and we had to cut my therapy prematurely to us feeling I was ready, but we agreed I was well enough and resilient enough not to be transferred to adult services. I "fell through the gap". I visited my sister in Miami after my treatment and spent eight weeks with her. While I was there, I put all of my techniques into practice, and I learnt how to care for myself. I gradually started to become healthy through eating well, walking to the beach every day, swimming and going to the gym. I began to see value in life again and feel peace when I stopped and took in the beauty of the world around me.

I then came back and started to spend time with friends. I went to a gig with a friend one evening when I was 17, and that was the night I met my now-husband, Chris. He was kind, warm and caring. We fell deeply in love and were married after eight months. However, we navigated a fractious and difficult beginning. Chris was in a band, and they expected a lot of his time and energy. However, I was also very dependent and sometimes my demons would envelop me, and I would seek Chris' care and attention. Chris didn't have any understanding of mental health issues and struggled to work out what he wanted and how he could help. I know he felt entirely powerless for a very long time, and he suffered because he couldn't take away my suffering, nor appease his friends. This resulted in a battle in Chris' mind. His bandmates and family felt that I was toxic, unstable and inadequate for him. Chris would sometimes heed their advice, and at times he left me, telling me he didn't love me. Other times he would be with me, and they would feel betrayed and angry at him. I felt their hate and lack of empathy, I felt every glare when I tried to mingle with them. They never asked me what it was like or how I felt. I would feel so anxious in their company that I would drink excessively, and then I would play into their assumptions that I was bad news. It was a perpetuating cycle that left me feeling ashamed and alone. Those beliefs I'd fought so hard to overcome began to be proven again, and despite being able to function in the world, they lay there underneath the skin.

Eventually, Chris made a commitment to be with me, and although things were rocky as a result, I gradually started to feel secure and loved. We then fell pregnant, and I think having a child growing inside me, that I knew would be my responsibility, accelerated my desire to heal. I felt so passionate about giving this baby a better future. I started my degree with The Open University in Psychology at this point. I studied while pregnant and learnt about child development. I learnt what childhood was supposed to look like, and I promised myself I would break the intergenerational trauma that came before me. I also dreamed of helping others who had suffered. I felt strongly about my experiences with accessing CAMHS and how difficult it was to access support. I was deeply called to draw on my experiences and use them to help others who suffered in the way I did. I knew that I would become a therapeutic practitioner, and I set my path to get there.

A few years later, I attended a Mindfulness-Based Cognitive Therapy course. By then, I had two little girls, aged 2 and 3. In this course, I learnt a new way of relating to my thoughts. It was only at this point that I realised that, despite being functional, I spent every day putting so much effort into challenging my thoughts, and that it was an exhausting process that I never quite succeeded in. At the time of my CAMHS therapy, I was taught about my "thinking errors" (this is an outdated term now and not at all the basis of CBT), and I had spent the rest of my years battling my faulty thoughts. Yet with mindfulness, through learning to unhook from the meaning of my thoughts, watch them, and develop a choice of whether to engage with them or not, I learnt that my thoughts weren't faulty at all. It was remarkable that gradually changing my relationship with my thoughts, and allowing them to be as they were, resulted in such a massive shift in the energy I was spending trying to make things different. Practising mindfulness was a difficult journey for me.

I learnt that I was so in my head, that I couldn't even feel my body. This is very common for people who have been sexually abused. I would lay to do a body scan, and I would feel nothing. Yet through practice, this changed. I started to feel my body, the heaviness of it. It was so remarkable. Yet it also filled me with deep sadness and grief. I recall weeping after I had done a 45-minute body scan because I felt so sad that I had consistently abused my body. Coming into a relationship with my body was hard, but it was such an essential part of my journey. I am now able to sit with strong emotions without my mind flying from them to protect me, something that was essential when I was endangered as a child, but which caused me suffering in adulthood. I can also use my body as an anchor; I can ground myself and feel safe. That had been transformational for me and continues to be so for my clients.

I continued my training alongside this and developed my skills as a practitioner. I feel that my own experiences enable me to feel deep empathy for my clients, and my skills as a reflective practitioner have allowed me to objectively separate my own "stuff" from my clients, while still feeling into their experience on an emotional level. I hope this makes me good at my job. Interestingly, I have studied research on mirror neurons, and theory shows that you have to have had an experience yourself for neuroimaging to light up the area in your brain that shows empathy. My mum used to say, "who feels it knows it", and this felt sense makes me so passionate about my job. I read a lot about compassion fatigue and burn out, and I can't imagine losing the fight in me to make other's futures better.

The most recent stage in my journey leads us up to now. I have seen a psychologist for Compassion-Focused Therapy (CFT), despite no longer having a mental health disorder. The interventions that I had had to date, including some counselling which became conducive to "analysis paralysis" (e.g. I sat in the room analysing myself out loud without coming to any understanding of what was underneath), didn't help me to make sense of my childhood. My therapist was fantastic, and we agreed to draw out a huge CFT based formulation. We spent session after session on this. It was hard work, and I had to go back to my past to really make sense of things and learn how everything fit together. But fit together it did, and it removed my shame because I could see exactly why and how things played out, and as my therapist said: "there were no other exit points for you". Formulation work is something that can be quite traumatic, but at this stage in my journey, I have felt empowered to take ownership of my story. To take back the power that I have always been at the mercy of. I now fully believe that nothing that occurred in my life, nor the way I have acted or felt, is my fault. That, in itself, has set me free. I remember turning up to a therapy session and saying "It's really, really weird. I feel like I'm a normal person. I have so much more energy, and I don't feel like I'm racing each day just to get to everyone else's start line". I know that there will be times in my life when my past brings up emotions and difficulties, but my understanding and the tools I have developed have led me not just to survive, but to thrive.

HOW AM I NOW?

It's a peculiar time to answer this question as I'm currently writing this while on lockdown during the coronavirus pandemic. It has actually been the perfect opportunity to put all the wisdom and tools I have learnt into practice. Lockdown has left me staring straight at my own reflection. There has been no hiding. Although this isn't unfamiliar territory, as I've become acquainted with my inner world in meditation, I have never had this much space. It's been tough, and things have certainly come up. Yet, I have held all of these difficulties in a container of compassion for myself. I have, mostly, chosen compassionate action when things have felt uncontainable. I have soothed myself and carried out acts with loving-kindness. I've let others comfort me, something I have struggled with during my life due to the deeply held belief that I don't deserve to be cared for. It feels like; strangely, I've been training for this moment my whole life. I am feeling a sense of acceptance for the situation, and I can see the small moments of wonder in amongst the fear that's being perpetuated by the discourse in the media. I'm not in denial about the seriousness, nor the tragedy around me, and I can feel the pain and suffering my human species is encountering. However, I've been able to witness my children's characters, to play with them and feel close. I've been able to sit at the window and feel the sun on my face while hearing the song of the native birds. They seem to be thriving while we're locked in, and that is beautiful. I've also had the opportunity to pause from my consistent desire to strive. Striving is something I have always battled with. Ironically, I have always strived to be better, and thus, never accepted where or who I am. In striving, there is no acceptance, and there is no love. Victories are short-lived before the next goal needs to be reached to fulfil my worth. Maybe the next distinction, or the next qualification, or the next project will portray my self-worth. Ironically, none of those things have enabled me to feel content within myself, not deeply. Yet here I have been proffered an opportunity to stop, to take stock, and to appreciate the small things. Admittedly, stopping has meant I have touched my own pain and bore the sorrows I have been running away from. Yet, this guiding hand has enabled me to really learn, experientially, that I can tolerate those emotions. They no longer control me, and I can bring kindness and compassion to those moments. So, to answer the question "How am I now?" I'd probably say, "I'm delightfully human, with all that comes with that".

WHAT DO I FEEL NEEDS TO CHANGE?

This question is interesting because it can be interpreted in multiple ways. Writing from the heart, I believe that what needs to change is society. I firmly believe that we are on that path. The #MeToo movement was profound. Additionally, many well-known figures and celebrities are now sharing their stories. I feel that we are silenced by shame and that this enables perpetrators to continue to abuse. That's why I'm adding my voice, for me and for every other person who was or is being sexually abused in childhood, wherever you are on your journey. You are not alone. We can own our stories, we can collectively heal our wounds, and we can change society.

WHAT HELPED ME?

If you would have asked me "what do you think will help you?" at the beginning of my journey, I undoubtedly would have said "love". I firmly believed that if someone would just love me, I would be healed. Being cared for has undoubtedly helped, but it has never filled the void, the emptiness. It sounds cliché, but it took me so many years to learn that until I had compassion for myself, everything else was a plaster over the wound. Things would work temporarily, but after a while, the plaster would wear, and the wound wouldn't be healed underneath. What has really helped is learning about myself. I have gained so much awareness through therapy and therapeutic practice, with each stage offering me a new jigsaw piece. It was the formulation work I recently carried out in partnership with my psychologist that enabled me to put all of those pieces together. It's been through seeing the full picture that I have been set free from the shackles of shame. However, if it had been early in my journey, and I hadn't had the pieces, it would have been premature to try and put those together. Ultimately, I guess what has helped me is my own determination to heal.

I would say it's my fearlessness in facing what scares me. Carl Rogers, an American psychologist, talks of this "actualising tendency". In his book, "A Way of Being", he talks about potatoes stored for winter in the disparaging conditions of his basement. He describes how they would grow shoots, despite not being in favourable conditions, and these would grow towards the light of a small window. Although they would never flourish, there is an innate drive to grow and to sustain life. Perhaps I started my life in those same disparaging conditions, but there was light in amongst the darkness, and I strove to find that light. Through therapy and the cultivation of that innate drive by people who have supported me, I've been able to find new conditions, and with that, I have flourished too.

WHAT DIDN'T HELP ME?

The initial experience of help-seeking was very damaging for me and even more damaging for people I have loved. My ex-boyfriend, who was also abused, had a similar experience in seeking help and subsequently lost hope in therapeutic support. This unfortunately ended tragically for him, and he died of a fatal drug overdose six years ago. Fortunately, despite my disillusionment, I remained receptive to being helped even after I was continuously being let down, and that was the best decision I could have made. More than that, I have now committed my life to remedy this. I currently work in early intervention for children and young people. The people I have helped, and continue to help, do not meet the threshold for CAMHS support. Through intervening early, I can ensure that so many young people do not feel rejected, and do not become disillusioned when they take the courageous decision to seek help. It is something I continue to remain passionate about.

THE BEST ADVICE I CAN GIVE SOMEONE GOING THROUGH MY TRAUMA

For all of you who have experienced childhood sexual abuse, it is not your fault. I can say that wholeheartedly. You do not need to hold onto the shame of your abuser, and you are worthy. My advice would be not to give up. I know it can feel like you are completely alone, and that things will never get better. I know it can feel like you are broken and will never be able to integrate into this world. I know you will fall into the trap of self-criticism and self-sabotage, and you will feel unworthy and unloved. I know that even reading this account, you will question what self-compassion is or how it's possible to obtain. It might also feel like an insult or feel too painful even to consider.

Healing is indeed a journey, and this short account cannot, by any means, portray the difficulty and pain in going through it. It's tender work, and it can feel impossible. Yet you are strong, resilient and brave, and you won't be going on this journey alone, all of us who have experienced abuse will be there holding your hand through it. You are beautiful, and I see you.

Ceridwen

I grew up in the North East of England. My family moved up from the West Midlands with my Dad's job when I was two years old. Newcastle is such a vibrant city edged wild countryside and filled with some of the warmest people you'll ever meet. We lived in a cul-de-sac on a relatively new estate, with loads of kids of different ages. We roamed the streets most evenings and weekends, riding our bikes, playing manhunt and waiting for the ice cream man to arrive. I loved living on my street.

As a kid, I was curious (which is a nice way of saying nosey) and liked to be included, which meant helping out even when I wasn't asked to. I ended up in the hospital a few times after breaking my big toe (dropping a can of tomatoes on it while unpacking the shopping) and getting a geranium leaf pulled out my nose ('d wanted to know how the furry skin felt inside my nostril).

I liked to do things by myself and practiced walking in secret. My parents used to watch me through the crack in the door. It was only once I had mastered it, that I paraded my 'sudden' gift by proudly walking from one side of the living room to the other. The perfectionist tendencies were there before I was even 2. Years later, in a corporate wellness workshop on vulnerability for one of the world's biggest companies, I made the mistake of revealing this story in the group sharing session. The facilitator leapt on it and in her New Jersey drawl, proclaimed "Well that says everything about you". Needless to say, I didn't stay at that company much longer.

I liked meeting people, and I loved being outside. I was always reading, drawing, I was in a swimming club, and I played the violin under duress. Yet as outgoing and friendly as I was, I was also incredibly stubborn, moody and lacking in confidence.

We'd been in Newcastle for a few years when my brother was diagnosed with Type 1 diabetes. He was just four, and I was six. This was back in the day when you had to inject insulin from tiny glass vials, and I often had to sit on him to hold him still while my mum injected him in tears. Having given him his insulin, my parents then had to measure out exactly the right amount of carbohydrate for my brother to eat and time meals so that he ate precisely an hour after his injection. Mealtimes with a small child are fractious enough without of having to make sure your kid eats all their pasta because they might hypo or die otherwise.

My mum saved all the calendars from when we were growing up. Filled with birthdays, trips out, appointments and visitors, 1987 - the year of my brother's diagnosis - is empty save the pre-written birthdays.

He was receiving a tremendous amount of attention at the time, which is when I started pretending to be ill at school. I don't remember doing it though apparently, it's a very common thing for children with unwell siblings to do. I used to say I felt sick or that I had a funny tummy. I knew I was loved and important at home. I just craved all the attention my brother was getting.

My parents thought it only fair we were treated the same so which meant low sugar Ribena, diabetic chocolate and mints. Since other kids were met with sweets after school, we had Sweet Day instead. On Saturdays, we were allowed to choose three sweets from the newsagents. There was no restriction on what we could have – if we wanted three Mars Bars, we could have them – and we could eat them whenever we wanted, which meant gorging the lot in front of Saturday morning kids' TV and then feeling sick until after lunch.

I was a chubby kid. Unlike the lithe, athletic and pretty girls on my street, I was podgy, stocky and awkward. Though tall for my age, I was constantly referred to as a 'big girl'. While I was lucky enough to have parents who never criticised my physical appearance, their love didn't stop the comments

We moved back to the West Midlands when I was 13. It was a tricky time as having been about to go into the final year of middle school, and I was now going into the second year of high school. I had my friends in Newcastle, I had my limited freedom of being able to go into town with them on my own, and I'd passed the entrance exam to go to a great high school in the city once I'd finished middle school.

Yet I was leaving all that behind to go to a school where everyone had already made friends. I was leaving a vibrant, buzzing city for a smaller, sleepier and altogether more stifling one. I was the new girl with a funny accent, at that awkward stage where puppy fat has yet to turn to curves. And I was a bag of hormones and rebellion and teenage angst on top.

Despite loving our new house with the fields behind it and beautiful light, I wasn't happy in my new city; I didn't feel like I belonged. Thanks to an enthusiastic new music teacher starting at the same time as I joined my new school, I was involved in music from my first day which helped me to make friends faster, even though I thought they were far less cool than the ones I had left behind. I fell in with a clique of girls who were all smart, musical and superior to anyone who wasn't in our gang. We all sang in the choirs and bands so hung out in the music room at lunchtime rather than with our peers, spent our weekends drinking in the park with older boys and went around thinking we were better than everyone around us.

Every few months, the ring leaders would choose someone in the group to ignore. My turn came when I was 14, and I was bullied for a year before it was someone else's go, and I was allowed back into the fold. Looking back, it was a good lesson as I learnt to toughen up, not take any crap and stand up for myself. But at the time, it was pretty grim. Thankfully, there was no social media back then, so the bullying stopped as soon as I left the school gates.

But it did my self-confidence no favours.

I knew I was bright, I loved school, I loved learning, and I felt like I could hold my own when it came to essays and exams. But when it came to how I felt about how I looked, the self-loathing was intense.

Even when I got to sixth form college and started going out with this cool skateboarder, I still used to get so anxious about going out, about what I was wearing, about how my body looked, about what was going to happen, that my Dad used to say he wished I wasn't going out at all.

While I was confident in my studies and amongst my friends, when it came to my appearance, I was ashamed. I hated what I saw in the mirror and slowly that self-loathing started to seep inside.

I was itching to go to university, desperate to get out of the dull city we had moved to, convinced that once at university, I'd find my tribe. Leaving my long terms boyfriend behind, I headed back up north, ready for my life to begin. But Sheffield was wet and grey, and I didn't immediately find my friends for life as all the movies had promised and I sunk into a deeper depression. I used to sit in my halls of residence, eating pate on toast and listening to The Archers on Radio 4. I should have been out there living it up. But I didn't feel like I deserved it. I didn't feel like my body deserved it. My beautiful aunt suggested I start swimming every day as that would give me a purpose and make me feel better. She emailed me every day without fail and looking back now, and I know those emails saved me on more than one occasion.

I made friends at university, but I was so serious about everything. Seriously obsessed with exercise and my diet though I never seemed to get any slimmer. Serious about my work. Serious about my extracurricular activities. I could never lighten up. The nagging doubts about my appearance prevented me from ever fully allowing me to let myself go and enjoy nights out. Instead, I carried this heavy sadness with me everywhere. And just like the rain, it started to seep in.

Quietly, this began to build up and cement itself inside me. I carried this sadness and self-loathing around for years. To New Zealand, Australia, across the far East, around Europe and back. I placed self-validation on others comments, what my on-off boyfriend thought of me, the jeans I could fit into, whether friends said I looked nice or not. Everything was external, external, external.

After travelling and working some temp jobs, aged 24, I'd landed a job working at my dream company. I had stalked them for a job for ages, and while the role itself wasn't quite what I wanted to do, I was so elated about getting the opportunity to work at such a cool place, I didn't really care.

The reality was very different. It was cliquey, like being back at school and in the loser group. Full of high achievers and Oxbridge graduates, the need to prove yourself was constant. I began to come in early and leave late, seeing as a badge of honour and proof of how committed I was to the company. Almost everyone there seemed to be living this hip London lifestyle. They were young, cool and gorgeous and no matter how hard I worked or how many things I volunteered for, I began to feel inadequate very quickly; like I was in the wrong place yet again.

I decided to train for the London Marathon with a couple of my workmates partly to be more involved in the company but mainly to lose weight. I lived in east London and work was in west London. So every day, I would get up in the dark at 5:30am, spend an hour underground as the Central line hurtled me across London, go for a training run before work, doing a full day's work and stay late to show willing, then leave in the dark, hustle back onto the packed tube and arrive home after 8:30pm every night. I had time to cook and eat before it was time for bed, and then the whole thing started over again. I was trying so hard to make a good impression at work, to fit in with the cool people I worked with, to stay fit, to lose weight, to be this glossy version of myself that I wanted to be. Instead, I was living to work. My weekends weren't filled with fun bars, gigs and parties. I never felt more alone in a city where I knew so many people.

I remember going for walks with this heavy sadness which by then had just become routine, numbing. I've since walked down those same streets and shuddered to think about how I ever let myself get that unhappy.

Plus I hated my job. My whole reason for being felt fake. I loved the company but hated what I was doing. Creative by nature, I was working in the commercial team where the numbers were like another language. I just wanted to be in the creative team but was told that was not going to happen.

I went home for Christmas that first year and spent most of it in bed with flu. My body, sensing that I was no longer in this fight or flight mode, seized the opportunity to heal all that I had been putting it through. I couldn't even eat dinner on Christmas Day.

But I got over it and caught up with friends, all keen to hear about my cool new London life. I went for walks with my family, I slept, I ate properly, and I started to feel better.

Within a week of going back to London, all the rest and rejuvenation had been quashed.

My birthday is at the end of January, and my parents came down to take me out for lunch. I'd booked us into this swanky fish restaurant and went to meet them at the train station. As they came along the platform at Paddington, carrying bags filled with presents and beaming, they scooped me up in a joint hug, and I began to cry uncontrollably.

I had no idea what was happening at the time. I couldn't stop the flow of tears or the deep, loud sobs emanating from my chest. It was only months later that I realised no one had touched me since I had been home for Christmas. Skin hunger is a real condition, and their burst of love made me realise just how lonely and unhappy I was.

My parents took me to a nearby pub, and as we sipped our pints of ale, they coaxed out of me just how unhappy I was. My Dad is a counsellor and suggested I should go and speak to somebody. They were both so brilliant that day, and I left feeling lighter and relieved that I didn't have to pretend everything was great when it wasn't.

I found an excellent clinical psychologist and CBT psychotherapist just down the road from where I worked. Over the next year and a half, she helped me figure out and narrow what was really going on with me.

In our first few sessions, she asked me to think about how I'd rate the following: my friends and family, my health, my home, my job and my love life. If three out of five were good, then I was doing pretty well. I had my friends and family; my health was fine. She pointed out that my love life was slightly different as that is something harder to have control over. Where I lived wasn't great, and I hated my job.

Having narrowed it down, my therapist suggested that it made more sense to change one thing at a time and see if that made a difference.

By that point, I was already out my shared east London flat and living with my best friends, a couple I'd known for years. My parents had called them after they'd seen me in London and asked if my friends would mind having me stay for a bit. The day before the London Marathon, I moved into a shared house in west London, a 15-minute bike ride to my job.

It became clear pretty soon after I moved that my job was the problem. So not long after, I quit. I quit with no plan of what I was going to do or where I was going to get money. I listened to myself properly and felt instantly better the minute I handed in my resignation. The funny thing was, as a result of handing in my notice, I ended up being offered the creative job there that I'd always wanted.

The counselling I had made me realise that good therapy isn't about being given the answers, and it's about being asked the right questions. Because once you're asked the right question, there is no avoiding the right answer for you. My therapist helped me to become kinder to myself, to recognise the beauty inside and out. She had me do things like a gratitude journal. She encouraged me to look at myself fully in a mirror instead of avoiding my thighs. She showed how my thoughts do not control me and that how I speak and address the world has a huge impact on who I am and how I see myself and others. Gradually, our sessions went from weekly, to fortnightly, to monthly. She never kicked me out or said: "That's it." She simply said on our last session "You can always come back whenever you need to". I went back a couple more times but it was clear to me by then, and I had the tools to get by.

It's not been plain sailing since then. I've made many mistakes, stumbled off the path and fallen back into old negative thought patterns. I just recognise those things for what they are now. No longer the perfectionist, I don't beat myself up anymore if I slip up.

Without sounding like one of those intensely spiritual people, I've come to find that happiness lies within. In fact, happiness is the wrong word. Contentment, acceptance, appreciation and peace - those are all internal, things that are far less transitory and fleeting than happiness.

And while I thought it sounded very cheesy at first, I've kept up the gratitude journal every day. Even if it's been a crap day or I'm tired or cross, finding things to be grateful for has made me more grateful by default.

I do what makes me feel good now. Meditation, swimming outdoors, reading, taking walks in the woods and by the sea, cooking.

I'm still learning to accept my body. Most days, I come out on top. The days I don't are the days I run myself a bath and watch a film in it with some good dark chocolate.

Tracking my menstrual cycle has been tremendous in understanding why some days I feel up and others I feel grotty. Hormones are a big part of one's emotional spectrum as a woman. Knowing I'm likely to have a wobble on Day 19 of my cycle makes me feel calm and more in control as it's as much to do with hormones as it is what's going on outside. This tracking has also helped me get more in touch with my body and the wonder that it is rather than a battle to fight. I can highly recommend Maisie Hill's Period Power as a fantastic practical guide to embracing what it is to be a woman.

While I was never one for taking drugs, I've stopped drinking alcohol, and that has helped my mental health immensely. Rather than numbing out, I now have to 'feel my feelings', and the funny thing is, the sooner I acknowledge them, the sooner I start to feel better.

However, of all the tools I have been shown and learnt, natural plant medicine is the one that has changed my life. I would go as far as to say that it has saved my life. What I have learnt and continue to learn about healing with plants and the power of this natural medicine has prompted me to study it to be able to help others experience the same benefits. I can think of no better occupation on this earth than helping others to help themselves. And in hindsight, I know that everything I have been through in my life has led me to this place. It's only now that I can be grateful for all that's happened; the good, the bad and the absolute rock bottom, floor weeping, unattractive ugly.

My hope for the future is to become a great healer, to have a home to call my own and to find someone to share my life with.

I feel lucky to be where I am today, even though writing this made me feel extremely sad to have spent so much of my life feeling miserable.

I've met some incredibly successful people over the years.

I've met famous writers, actors, politicians, musicians, chefs and tech wizards.

Billionaires, millionaires, people you think have got it all sorted.

I've met men and women who have graced the covers of magazines, billboards and catwalks for some of the world's most famous brands.

To learn that even these people, the ones society regards as the beautiful people had the same body issues, self-loathing and hang-ups and insecurities as me, was revelatory.

It made me realise that deep down, we are all the same. We all want to be loved, recognised and accepted. Suffering is part of the human condition.

To be human is to suffer.

But to be human is also to heal and grow from the adversity's life throws at us.

To suffer some more and then heal and grow and so on.

Cliched perhaps but none the less true for its ubiquity. No one is perfect.

No one is meant to be perfect.

We must be kind to ourselves and each other, whenever and however we can.

Claudia

I grew up in Worthing, West Sussex, right on the beautiful South Coast with my Mum, my Dad and my sister, who's 18 months younger than me.

Living in the location I do has always been something I'm lucky to have; as I lived a 30-minute walk from the beach and just on the edge of the South Downs National Park. It's something I appreciate now as it helped me to cope with my mental health, just being able to take a walk or a run in the fresh air, out in nature. Simply wonderful.

Growing up, ever since I have been able to stand on my own two feet, (which I was very late doing: a possible giveaway to my difficulties?) whether it be the way I used to react to situations or had social contact with others; I knew that I was different. I would never quite understand why, until many years and dramatic twists and turns later the real reasons why this was the case.

From as early as I can remember, I had always struggled to "fit in" and to find my place amongst others my age. I guess as a 4-year-old when girls are playing with dolls and boys and playing with cars, and you were playing with puzzles- completing them in rapid times, I was an outcast.

This continued into my school life, and I became socially excluded from many classes. Nobody wanted to sit next to me, Nobody noticed that I was struggling- and this built up into increased anger that was more and more difficult to control.

I would lash out and get angry because I didn't understand why nobody would speak, play or help me to make friends. I was labelled as a naughty child and sent to anger management therapy at the age of 8- which I got kicked out of for being angry (ironic, right?); when I didn't understand how to express my emotions properly.

So I then got to high school, and at this time things at both school and home were difficult, I wouldn't speak for days unless spoken to and would eat in my bedroom or the toilets at school. I was physically and emotionally bullied at school by both students and teachers (yes, really). I remember one teacher said to me that "you will never get anywhere so you might as well give up and kill yourself". (That was just one of the things said to me- but some were a lot, lot worse.)

This upset me and sent me into such a low mood that I began to self-harm.

So I finished school and got okay grades. I kept my head down, got on with my work and then it was time for college. Through all of this, I was still self-harming every day but covering it up so nobody would see the pain I was in.

I went to college, and it felt strange - as for the first time in my life, I felt accepted, acknowledged and as I mattered. All of this was so strange to me as I'd never felt like this before. I'd never been surrounded by people who "helped me to fit".

It was such an extreme shock and a change, and at the time, I couldn't deal with it. I felt awful for being liked; I felt anxious about fitting in 'naturally'.

This was when I realised "I don't deserve sadness, I don't deserve happiness, I don't deserve anything.". That's when the thoughts of suicide came in, and I saw no point in living.

It was May 2014, and I had reached a point where I couldn't take it anymore. I felt like I didn't deserve to be liked or accepted by anybody. I felt like I had no way out apart from to attempt suicide.

I was adamant, and I was going to do it. Nobody would find me; nobody would care. Nobody would be able to help me; so I'd have to help myself and end my life, but I was found and was then taken to a psychiatric hospital where I spent around six months. It was tough in there, but I realised that people did care and that I would try my best to get better to a point where I could feel happy. Not all the time, but happy enough to realise that my life was worth living, and I had a purpose.

So when I was discharged from the hospital, I started back at college and undertook a course in theatre production. I wanted to be creative and learn to express myself through the theatre arts.

During this course, just before my 19th birthday, I was given a diagnosis of Autism- and things finally clicked. I knew why I was different and felt like it wasn't my fault and that it was just a part of me. It meant I saw and processed the world differently, and that was okay.

I enjoyed the theatre course and wanted to continue this so enrolled at a University in London to study theatre technologies.

Moving to London was a big move for me, but I knew that if I wanted to prove to myself and those who had doubted me in the past that I could make something of my life; then I had to be willing to age steps to improve myself and prove them and myself wrong.

University was fantastic; I made so many friends and felt so wonderful to be accepted for being who I was- not just my diagnosis or my bad days, but I knew there was something. Issuing- like I didn't just have Aspergers Syndrome, that there was something more. I got through the first year, and it was in my second year that I was diagnosed with Anxiety, depression and OCD alongside the Autism. I finally felt like I was able to be my authentic self too. So, at the beginning of my third year of university, I came out as non-binary; which means I identify as being neither female or male. I finally felt like I was able to be myself- to be Claudia. To be, simply me.

Now I've graduated with a first-class Bachelors of Arts degree in theatre technologies with Honours, and I've moved back home to do teacher training to become a theatre teacher at college and university level to inspire the next generation of young people to be creative and express themselves through the performing arts to achieve their potentials. I am looking at doing a masters course too and seeking to be an inclusive arts practitioner to run workshops for those with mental health conditions to get creative.

SO WHAT HELPS ME TO COPE WITH DAILY LIFE?

I am labelled too complex by healthcare professionals to receive any 'official' mental health support, but I have taken my recovery into my own hands.

One of the most important tools in my toolbox (being a theatre artist, I like to use analogies- because why not?!) is running. I'm not a fast runner and I don't do long distances either. But when I run, I feel free. I feel like I can get those endorphins up without having to resort to self-destructive behaviours like self-harming.

Another massive thing that helps me is the ability to create art. I love using technology and combining this with theatre performance to make works of art that offer an insight to others into what life is like in my world with both a learning disability and truthfully though, the support form others like my friends and family has been so beneficial and helped me realise that I have the potential to do whatever I want to do, be whoever I want to be. Speaking up when I am struggling, talking at events run by members of the growing mental health community on both a local and national level; doing podcasts, writing blogs. All of the support I get from my support network is wonderful. We all help each other realise we are not alone, and it's okay to be different.

WHAT ADVICE WOULD I GIVE SOMEBODY FOR THE FUTURE?

The most significant bit of advice I would give somebody for the future would be to find something that works for you when you are struggling. There is no one size fits all 'cure' to mental health, and it is okay to be on medication, it is alright to be in therapy, it is okay to do whatever works for you.

The other bit of advice I would give is to speak up- even if you don't know the words. Get creative with the way you express your emotions, and it could be through drawing, music, poetry or journaling. Just don't suffer in silence.

One wish for the future would be that mental health and the stigma surrounding what it means to have depression, or anxiety, or OCD, or Autism, or any diagnosis is that these labels do not define the person. We need to work to eradicate the stereotypes and seek to educate the world as to what they really mean for the individual.

I can only speak from my experiences, and I'm gaining more and more confidence every day in my abilities. I still have bad days, but I hold onto and remember the good days I have. I try to strive to achieve my potential and be the most authentic version of myself every day. It's okay not to be okay, but it's not okay to struggle and face it on your own.

Chris

I was bullied as a kid. Weak and always ill, I was four months premature and had a tracheotomy. So had a hole in my neck until 12 I think. My Mum was always taking amphetamines and stealing money from our birthday cards and stuff so that might have had something to do with it?

I honestly don't know what triggered it, it just developed. I didn't like my job, and I didn't get on with my stepdad, he would tell me just to do a mundane job I didn't want to do, and my dad would encourage me to do my dream jobs. But my stepdad would instantly shoot anything down and tell me to grow up.

I was 19. It started with depression, extremely low mood and anxiety. Eventually, I started seeing shadow's out of the corner of my eye and hearing occasional noises with no explanation. I put this down to my lack of sleep, nightmares, and stress at work in a job I hated.

I went to a Dr to ask for help and get some answers, they were accommodating and told me to keep a journal, which I did, and they would set me up with an assessment with a specialist which would then turn into regular visits at my home, which I shared with my Mum and step Dad.

My Mum was a selfish drug addict/alcoholic who would stay awake for days on end going through my bedroom looking for money or alcohol to steal or be sleeping off a hangover for three days.

And my stepdad didn't understand and would corner me and say things like "when are you going to start acting normal?" And "I don't like you being here because I think you're going to run a knife across me and your mum's throat" and would lose his temper when I'd ask to have the front room to myself for 20 minutes when the home visits would happen.

This caused me to ignore the visits in fear of my stepdad losing his temper with me, which caused me to lose control of my grip on reality in a matter of a few days.

I would be woken up every morning at 4 am by a figure I would call Rob. He was a tall bearded man with animal pelt sewn onto the top half of his face, with an animal pelt poncho almost covering his entire body.

And I would just sit outside on a bench and talk to him, and he would give me confidence and would tell me how to go about changing my life and becoming a physically and mentally stronger person.

One day I answered the door to the home visit nurses and confided in them that I was at a real low point, explained how I would see and hear this person, and I was contemplating suicide.

I got sectioned that night and put into the local hospital. I was put on new, stronger medication that night, which made me feel sick. So, I couldn't stomach eating anything that night. Not to mention, I didn't have much faith in being able to walk into a dining room full of people I didn't know and not fall over anything or into anyone.

This made the nurses think I had an eating disorder, so I would be heavily encouraged to eat to the point it got irritating.

One evening, this one patient in the unit got hold of a pair of scissors and began scratching the faces off of the Dr's staff board while screaming "He's a lying cheating bastard."

She then ran towards me; I was propping myself up against a doorframe unable to move with much coordination, so I pulled a sofa in front of me, causing her to fall over it and injure herself.

I would get in trouble for this and get labelled with "violent outbursts" and got given a lot more medication on top of what I was already taking.

I remember my dad would drive 100 miles after work from his city with my sister, to come and visit me, this became all I would look forward to throughout the day. (This again put things into perspective for me as my Mum who lived a mile barely away would visit me twice in 2 months, and my stepdad wouldn't visit me at all)

Only this time my Nan came along to visit too. And the new pile of medication I was on, kicked in. I was looking at my Nan talking to me, and I felt my face began to stiffen up in an angry expression. My Nan thought it was funny, thinking I was just getting annoyed with what she was talking about. I ran to the toilet and ran my face under the warm water to try and regain control of my face, but it didn't help. They then decided to take me down to the hospital cafe, and I could feel my face stiffening into a look of pure rage. But I couldn't control my face muscles.

We then decided to come back to the unit, and my dad was talking to me, and he looked down at my chest with a look of confusion, I followed where he was looking, and my arms had stiffened up like a praying mantis and my hands were contorted. I couldn't push them back down at all. Then over the next 10 minutes, I was struggling to walk, my jaw was locked, and the right side of my face was stuck open showing my teeth and my neck was twisting to the right so far that I was worried it was going to break.

My Nan became visibly upset which shocked me as I've never really seen her be anything but a strong Irish woman, so I tried comforting her but just made the situation worse by stroking her arm with my T. rex hands and trying to say "don't worry nan I'll be okay" but just spat on her through my exposed teeth.

I was worried as I thought I was stuck like this forever, but they eventually gave me another green tablet which made me fall asleep, and I woke up able to move again.

After having the new girl, unaware that I had only been this way for about an hour, ask me if I would like to come on a fun run...

I was eventually allowed out with regular visits from a woman who I would just call my nurse. She would check in on me every day and make sure I was taking medication and eating correctly. And she would encourage me to keep writing in my journal. Which I would, writing down dream's id had and dark thoughts.

One day, my Mum, while rooting around my bedroom, found my journal and read every page of it.

She then called my dad up and attempted to read it over the phone to him, but he stopped her and scolded her for invading my privacy.

She became focused on one entry I'd written, which I'd said about a time my dad had become agitated and lost his temper with me. It scared me because I was a child. But as an adult, it wasn't that big of a deal. She homed in on this and would call my dad with drunk rants and attempt to make him feel guilty for my illness.

She then showed my stepdad everything is written down, and I remember it being 5 am, he stormed in my room and pulled me out of my bed. Shouting at me about everything I was writing, and how he didn't trust me not to kill them, and that I was just faking it all and being lazy.

He made me get dressed and kicked me out of the house.

I remember as I left, my Mum was in bed and I heard her on the phone to my sister telling her what was happening, for some reason my nephew was awake and on the phone at the time, and I heard her say "You're not a liar like your uncle Chris, are you?"

It was about 5:10 am, snowing, and I had nowhere to go. So, I just wandered around, I made it into the local town centre and decided to follow this river for about a mile. I found a little spot between 2 sets of trees and I just sat, crying then getting angry then thinking I was in the wrong until around 8 am when I texted my nurse. She scolded me for not calling as soon as I got kicked out, but I didn't want to wake her up.

She then came to see me, bought me some breakfast and talked me round to going back home, now my stepdad was at work, to try and sort things out with my Mum.

She was just shouting from upstairs that I was the one who wanted to leave home, and she can't believe after all the help she's given me that I'm walking out.

So, I left, and my nurse put me in a B&B.

I stayed here for about a week until I got moved into a youth hostel the next town over.

My first night there I called my dad up, who was furious about me being kicked out. But was even more furious with the fact that my room didn't have a kettle so I couldn't make myself a cup of tea.

So the next day, he turns up outside the youth hostel with a brand new kettle, bags of food fresh bedclothes, and my Nan is with him, she gives me about 15 little plastic tubs of this fantastic yellow rice and chicken that she knew was my favourite and used to cook for me when we would go and visit.

He gave me some money to tide me over with rent and always promised to help me as much as he could.

This was about as good as my stay in the hostel got, everyone in the hostel was on ketamine, amongst other drugs. And were up all hours of the night screaming, arguing, getting into fights with each other. I tolerated it for about two weeks until I caught someone trying to break into my room, so I packed up everything I had into a rucksack, and I walked out.

I went back to the original spot I'd found when I was first kicked out, I managed to find an abandoned tent and put that in one of the small forested areas by the river, and I stayed here for about a year, I'd lie to everyone and tell them I was okay and getting on well. Met with my nurse who I would lie to and say I just liked being here during the day.

I'd go to the library and read up of bushcraft survival, I learned how to make snares and how to track animals, so I'd survive off squirrels and rabbits I'd catch in snares, and fish I would catch out of the lake with an old piece of fishing line and hook I found on the river bank. And I was genuinely happy like this. I was by myself. Unfortunately, I'd also stopped taking my medication, so I was seeing visions of Rob again, which was a form of company which I didn't mind too much.

One day I went to visit my nurse, and she was visibly worried about me, telling me I'd lost weight and was too skinny, and politely telling me that I didn't smell too great. I apologised and said I'd go home and shower, but she followed me back to my campsite and demanded I go back to the youth hostel.

I then got moved from the second floor, down into this bedroom directly in front of the office, where I stayed for about three months until they moved me into the hallway house programme.

I got moved with this wannabe gangster who would sell drugs out the front door to the local gang of morons, then get annoyed why people were breaking into the garden and stealing his weights they were all using that day.

I'd also made friends with this girl who would come and visit her dad a few doors down from me, and we would go for walks and hang out. She introduced me to some of her friends, and we all became close.

One night I remember waking up to the door being banged on and hearing loads of shouting downstairs, I ran down the stairs half awake and in my boxers, to a group of men in balaclavas, one of them had my housemate against the wall and was relentlessly punching him in the face, I glanced back upstairs. I hallucinated Rob upstairs smiling at me almost encouraging me to fight, but I got spotted by one of them guarding the open front door who yelled at me to get on the floor, so I yelled: "fuck off and get the fuck out of my house."

I pulled the other one off my housemate by the collar of his coat and got him outside and slammed the front door.

By this time my hallucinations were getting even worse, so I called my nurse up that morning who started the conversation up with the good news that a house I'd bid on was accepted and I was moving into it within the next few weeks.

It just happened that the flat I was moving into was next door to the girl I'd made friends with a few weeks before.

I moved in and got away from all the trouble where I used to live; everything was going well.

My neighbour invited me to her birthday gathering she was having; our friends were going, so I thought why not.

I'd met up with a group of friends about 3 hours before the party in this field; we were having some beers and talking when a group of the local troublemakers approached us. They started trying to trade beers with us and then tried to get one of my friends to sniff a line of god knows what with him.

One of them spotted me, and I knew I recognised him from somewhere, and he said to me "I know you; you were that crazy one from school."

So, we had a bit of a laugh and a catch-up, and they eventually walked away.

We then made our way to the party, and it was going great. We'd set some tents up, and we're having a pleasant time with a small group of friends. Then the group of idiots from earlier turned up. They decided to come and sit with us and were being polite; then I couldn't find a couple of my friends I'd come with.

I sat in my friends' tent trying to text him when the idiot from earlier sat next to me and said something along the lines of "yeah you're like me, you look mad, and everyone assumes you're trouble, but really trouble just finds you, earlier I had these two people come up to me and start on me."

My phone then rings, and it's my friend, he's out of breath telling me the guys we saw earlier threatened him and told him he wasn't allowed back to the party, and that him and another of our friends were sitting in a field about half a mile away.

I then grabbed the guy out of the tent and told him that he better come with me and apologise to the people he threatened.

I packed the tent up the best I could in 10 seconds and walked over to where my friends said they were.

The guy I took with me apologised, and they shook hands, and he left.

I remember seeing Rob again behind my friends smiling at me.

I then turn around to see him run towards a group of about 30 of his friends, and they all ran towards me.

I thought "oh fuck, I'm dead."

And get hailed with punches and kicks so in a blind panic I started swinging punched and grabbed someone, pulling them to the floor, and I remember, I got kicked in the head, so I pushed the person head into the ground as hard as I could and bit his nose.

This was the biggest mistake I made because now everyone then knew something was up. Every time I would go out to the pub with my friends, I would have to get into a fight because someone would want to see if they could fight with the local psychopath. You'd get into a fight with one person, and his friends would then come after you as retaliation, so on and so on.

Some of my friends would begin to ask me to go with them to go and collect money people owed them, and if they were getting started on outside of a pub, they'd always call me, and I'd have to go and sort them out.

This made me eventually lose any form of confidence I had, I liked the idea of being intimidating having been bullied relentlessly at school, but it got annoying having to look over your shoulder every time you went out.

I realised this is what the manifestation of Ron way; he was all my fears of being a victim. He would encourage me to perform violent or threatening acts on others so that I wouldn't be able to be hurt by them.

I began to reply on whiskey; I'd drink it every day, I'd drink myself into a hole so I could get some sleep.

I had tried sleeping tablets but coupled with my constant nightmares; they would trap me in sleep for hours.

This, coupled with my psychosis and depression, spiralling out of control I sort of snapped into the idea that I was going to end it. I tried to take my own life.

Again, the person who helped me here was my dad; he would call me at least three times a day to check in on me. And when he didn't hear from me for three days, he said he knew something was wrong.

He got one of my sisters to drive my Mum down to my flat where they found me on the sofa.

I woke up in the hospital unable to talk; I was lashing out at everyone and punching anyone who came close to me.

It turns out I was on ICU in a coma for a few weeks before I woke up.

It was a real eye-opener for me and made me realise how much the people who care about you come through.

My dad sister Melissa and Nan are the best family I could ever hope for.

And since then I'm now married to a beautiful wife Emily who's everything I could ever hope for in a person.

It's taught me my coping methods when I feel down and depressed, and I've always got people I know are going to be there at a moment's notice.

Dalila

I genuinely believe that I was born with anxiety.

My Mother was the daughter of Algerian immigrants. She was born in France, and they were living in the worst poverty. Her Mother died giving birth to her 6th child when my Mother was only one years old.

My Mother's childhood was like a Dickens novel, Orphanage, constant physical and verbal abuse and living with a stepmother from hell.

She got married at 17 to escape this harsh childhood, but her anxiety never left her, and she passed it out to her children. My Mother was a big worrier, often worrying for nothing, and I sadly learnt to do the same.

I remember as a child having strong palpitations, but at the time, I never knew exactly what the meaning of these palpitations were.

My parents divorced when I was 8, and my dad never really took care of us.

My brother, who also had mental health issues, started to abuse me verbally and sometimes he was very violent, and I was living with anxiety always.

I learnt how to deal with this condition over time, but my emotions were very up and down, and during my teenage years, I tried to end my life many times to simply just try and stop the pain.

I felt useless and a burden and a constant inner battle with very low periods sometimes.

Times helped, and I got better, and I can now look back and thank God that I failed, as I have a beautiful daughter and an amazingly supportive husband who mean the world to me.

Three years ago, everything turned for the worst, and my Mother died from cancer, and I decided to have a preventative double mastectomy to prevent the same fate.

While I was recovering from this major surgery, I went into conflicts with my employers.

They allocated me a new manager who was very inexperienced and very intrusive, and she organised many meetings and doctor's appointments to be able to get some adjustment.

Not only my privacy was not respected, but they treated me as someone who had simply just opted for cosmetic surgery.

They declined any adjustment on my challenging timetable, but they were offering better rosters to staff who had no medical issues. They even lied to prove that I was faking my physical pain and fatigue.

I started to feel a burden again and was so overwhelmed that the suicide thoughts came back.

I thought about my daughter and I went to the GP. I was diagnosed as severely depressed.

I started antidepressants for the first time. After one month, I tried to come back to work, but they tried to ban me for psychological reasons. I was not a safety issue for anyone at work.

I managed to come back after alerting my union, and during this time, my employers were promoting mental health awareness.

Last December, my little brother got murdered. He was only 31. I became completely numb and totally unable to express myself since then, and it has been hard to cope, but with the antidepressants, my emotions are stuck. I have this feeling of not being able to grieve. I'm still shocked and unable to process this loss. Four days after he died, my employers replied to my tribunal claim. They denied that I have a physical impairment and were challenging my claims with false allegations. Everything seemed just to hit me at the same time, which was hard.

HOW YOU ARE NOW

I'm preparing my preliminary for the tribunal, with a total fear and anxiety and I live day by day. I do now see a counsellor, to be able to release my anxiety and grieve my brother. The counsellor also encouraged me to grieve my old body, as I was not allowed to do that in the best conditions.

WHAT YOU FEEL NEEDS TO CHANGE?

Hypocrisy about the stigma and people promoting mental health issue by opportunism.

People need to learn how to be kind and treat each other with respect.

WHAT HELPED YOU? MY DAUGHTER AND MY HUSBAND.

My Mother was my shield, and she always made sure that I was doing better.

Even that she was a very anxious person, her strength during her cancer was incredible.

She is no longer here, so I learned to be stronger.

WHAT DIDN'T HELP YOU?

The way people perceive me from the outside, people think that I'm coping well.

Mental stigmas are not always obvious.

People who are the most distressed don't always show it.

THE BEST ADVICE YOU CAN GIVE SOMEONE GOING THROUGH YOUR TRAUMA?

The best advice is to be surrounded by people who matter the most.

With time, you learn who is genuine, but unfortunately, not many people have got your back, so choose wisely who you can trust and confide in.

Meditation and doing activities which all can help you feel better as somedays I just wanted to stay in my bed or lay on my sofa all day.

My child is my world, and what matters the most to me and without her, I would struggle to cope.

My daughter gives me the strength to get up every day, and I am really trying to make sure that she won't feel the same and that my past and my present won't affect her.

Dan

I was always a quiet child, lacking in confidence, except in certain circumstances – playing football, or on stage in school plays. I felt I was intelligent, but for whatever reason was not confident about my looks. I was fortunate to come from a supportive and loving family background and cannot blame my parents. My parents always have been, and continue to be the most caring, loving and supportive parents you could ever wish for.

This was compounded when I went to secondary school, Skinners Grammar School for Boys, as much as I tried to fit in, I didn't, I was bullied horrendously, every morning, I would walk into my classroom, to be bundled by the entire class, they didn't do it to anyone else, just me. This continued for about a year (in their opinion, "the school doesn't have a bullying problem") until I finally changed schools, but by then the damage was already done.

I became a timid, self-conscious person; when I reached my late teens, I struggled immensely. If I got to the pub before my friends, I couldn't just sit calmly and wait, I felt out of place, so turned to the fruit machines, in a twisted way, they gave me a sense of purpose.

I knew I was only hurting myself, but through distorted thinking, it allowed me to be in a social setting, but without needing to be brave enough to speak to people. I did have friends but rarely felt part of the inner circle, but in reality, I was the one putting up the barriers.

As time went by, my gambling became all-encompassing, its truth, I had given up on myself as a person and on my dreams. I got bored in various jobs, and so continuously took sideways steps, never progressing, in my mind, I would never be able to do normal things like own a house because it was always going to be out of my financial reach.

I could lose a month's wages in a couple of days, knowing what I was doing was wrong, and tearing myself apart, but once the money was gone, it was a relief, I was back in my comfort zone of failure.

More than anything, I wanted to be a Dad, but how could I be? I couldn't look after myself, who could ever love me? I wished I was dead; the only thing that stopped me was not wanting to hurt my family. I thought of many ways to take my own life, leaving everyone to assume that it was a tragic accident?

My life had been over in my mind for years.

This continued until I was 29, at which point, I was for the first time lucky, I entered Gordon House, a residential treatment centre, with a nine-month programme.

I was not allowed to work, and instead attended a range of different counselling sessions, both group and individual.

What was special about this time in my life, was that I was allowed to take a prolonged period, in which to understand who I was, who I wanted to be, and what was important to me.

I'm not going to say it was easy, but for a long time, I could honestly say it was the best time of my life, supported by similar people, who could understand where I was coming from, and where I was going. They just got it.

I guess I was fortunate enough to have those thoughts that many people are experiencing today, during the lockdown period, the chance to pause and take a look at myself and what I needed to change to give me the life I wanted.

Where am I today, some thirteen years further forward? Well, I'm sat at home, one that I own, with the knowledge that my wonderful loving wife, is sat cuddling my two-year-old daughter, while my amazing stepdaughter Abi is working hard on her schoolwork.

I'm in a good position mentally, despite struggling financially with the Coronavirus lockdown, both my wife and I decided that we needed to change careers and elected to go self-employed at the start of the year, so don't get any financial support. I have learned that if I am unhappy, then I have the power to take control and make the changes that I need – life is too short.

I understand that I cannot change the rules, and instead, I take the view that I am lucky to have this extra time to do things like go for a family walk across fields with my girls – we have imposed a no phones run and enjoy each other's company.

I guess I am comfortable with who I am; I don't need fast cars or big houses to give me validation and a sense of worth.

As a wise man (My Dad) once told me (well, actually a lot more than once), "Life is all about choices" – and I choose to be happy and to live my life to the best of my abilities.

The biggest single thing that didn't help me was being frequently told "Just stop" – as if the thought had never crossed my mind. Mental health and recovery is a journey, with ups and downs, I also had to accept that I needed to lose the extremes – both the highs and the lows, and accept who I am to be who I needed to be.

The best advice I would give someone is to accept that they do have choices, although they might not be easy, or seem available. Sometimes you have to take the scenic route to get to where you want and need to be. If you need to take time out to get yourself back on track do it, there is a benefits system here for a reason, and you will be a better you if you need to stop working while you heal yourself.

Giving up isn't always failing, recently I decided to leave not only my job, but my career and retrain to do something that I wanted, and this was for my health and happiness. Was I giving up, or simply making a change to improve myself and make me a better Dad and husband?

In my experience there are no right or wrong answers, what works for me may not work for you, but always remember, people do care, and they will help and support you, often more than you know.

Now it's over to you to take the first step in your recovery, don't give up on yourself, I haven't.

Graham

My name is Graham. I'm 51 years old and suffer from PTSD, Anxiety and Depression.

I was born in a bathtub in Tunbridge Wells to a standard white middle-class family. My childhood was no different to anyone else, and hours were spent in the fresh air playing and talking with friends, unlike in today's world of social media and gaming.

In hindsight, my struggle with mental health began when I met my first wife, although it has taken me 20 years to realise this. Her father sexually abused her for several years as a child, which she made clear at the start of our relationship. He was over 6-foot-tall, 20 stone and an ex grenadier guard, a very aggressive and imposing person. He was very controlling and used to follow us when we started dating, no matter where or how far we went. His mood swings were a thing to be very wary of, so I always had to judge every meeting or encounter with him.

The dating went well, and we decided to get married, and this is where my life started to take a turn for the worse. Up until our marriage she had been very easy going and a lovely person, but this changed as soon as we were on honeymoon where a temper and controlling personality suddenly appeared. This shocked me to such an extent that I remember being curled up in a ball in tears, scared and wondering if I had made a huge mistake. What followed was 14 years of emotional and physical abuse and living in fear while being controlled by my wife. The control was to such an extent that she didn't even tell me she had stopped taking the contraceptive pill until she was pregnant. This happened twice, and I now have two beautiful daughters who were my focus and my world during the 14 years of abuse. Looking back, it is clear that part of me shut down and I was suffering from depression, but I had no idea at the time because my daughters were my world and my brain was blocking out the bad stuff. My life was walking on eggshells 24 hours a day.

During this period, both of my daughters were sexually abused by their maternal grandfather. I walked into a room and discovered it happening. He received a 12-year prison sentence. There was no anger or emotion from me at that point towards him, and all feelings were suppressed because, in my mind, I had to put my daughters first.

After 14 years, my first wife told me that our marriage was over, in reality, releasing me from the emotional and physical abuse.

For the next five years, I simply existed, thinking that if I could survive that experience, nothing else could be that bad. I considered myself a very chilled and relaxed person and prided myself in never getting angry or frustrated.

I then met my second wife, Debbie, who loved me for who I was, treated me as a human being and gave me happiness. I didn't think possible. It was at this point that my world collapsed.

Debbie started to notice a change in me, despite the fact that I was happier than I had ever thought possible. The events of my previous marriage were beginning to catch up with me, and I spiralled into a complete nervous breakdown. The day it happened was the scariest day of my life, my blood ran cold, I had pins and needles and couldn't function even at the basic level. My marriage collapsed as a result which just added to the pain I was going through, as I had lost a beautiful, caring and wonderful woman who had given me such happiness. I still love Debbie very much and hold no ill feelings towards her at all. This was my fault because I hadn't seen the signs or sort help during my first marriage and instead had suppressed a lot of emotions and feelings. I thought I was strong and in control to have survived the constant abuse, but I was actually broken, and it took several years to surface, but when it did, it destroyed the happiest time of my life.

Eighteen months later, I am still receiving counselling and every day is a struggle. I am on antidepressants and tablets for my anxiety. While counselling allows me to talk about my experiences, and it is important to do so, it doesn't give me any coping mechanisms.

I work for a big Bank as a Learning and Engagement manager, writing and delivering training material. Working is my coping mechanism as I have to be positive and fun while training people and am lucky that I love the job I do. I am also responsible for the wellbeing and have focused, not surprisingly, a great deal on mental health. I talk openly about my own experience when it is appropriate to do so in a workshop, and the delegates are stunned because they see me as a happy, fun, jokey and positive person. Had they seen me outside of work, they would have seen a very different person.

I HAVE LEARNT A NUMBER OF THINGS OVER THE PAST FEW YEARS:

- It is not a strength to suppress your emotions – they will come back and bite you
- A basic understanding of mental health and what to look for would have helped me
- I am not alone in feeling this way
- Talking does help–it is nothing to be ashamed of
- Exercise is a great distraction
- Take one day at a time, don't beat yourself up if you have a bad day
- Shutting yourself off from friends, while understandable, is very damaging
- Focusing on the good things in your life does help.

If I have one piece of advice, it would be to talk to someone that has been through it too. Counsellors do a valuable job as they understand how the mind works, but I struggled to connect because they hadn't actually experienced what I am going through.

The day I met Jenny changed my life, she understood me, got where I was coming from, and there was an instant trust in her. To see someone that has been through such a dark time but be able to have a smile that lights up a room gives me hope for the future.

As I write this, we are in the midst of the Coronavirus Crisis and my coping mechanism has been taken away from me as I now have to work from home, I am scared about the next few weeks and how I will cope. I know I am not alone in feeling like this.

I still have very low self-esteem and am still grieving over my breakup with Debbie but thanks to Jenny I have hope now that this will change. It is a marathon not a sprint but thanks to Jenny there is now a light at the end of the tunnel. I will keep talking about my emotions and trying to embrace them and will continue to encourage others to do the same.

Joseph

The biggest thing I have learnt about having depression and anxiety you have to talk about it.

When I was first diagnosed with this illness, I was highly embarrassed, should men actually suffer from these demons? The answer is, yes!

I have a friend in their 60's who suffers from it, which came to a complete surprise. He has a great life- Nice car, beautiful house, a very successful business and two children. I thought what is there to be depressed about when you have what most people dream of! Well, this proves you don't know what people go through behind closed doors.

I took my first anti-depressants when I was 23, and to this day at the age of 26, I am still on them.

I grew up with an alcoholic, homophobic father who treated both my brother and I totally different.

While I was growing up, I actually experienced a lot of homophobic abuse throughout school and my teenage years. When I was 16, I was spat on outside a restaurant for being gay, verbally abused at work and even beaten up. However, I am very good at defending myself- Mum always said I don't take any prisoners!

It wasn't till my early 20's my mental health started taking its toll on me. I think it was everything catching up with me.

My head is a very complex thing. I wake up daily not knowing what mood I will be in- will it be a good day or a low day?

My low days are the worst; it's like having this black cloud over you and can't remove it. When I have a day like this, I can't make conversation, think or even find the positives.

I have even had suicidal thoughts, who would miss me anyway until I meet with my family and friends then those thoughts go away.

Every day, you go past many people, and you have no idea what they are going through. If you say something to the wrong person when they are in a sensitive state of mind, it may be the last thing they hear and take their own life, I have experienced that.

I think some people don't understand how difficult it is, living with mental health illness. I hate about it, I feel that I burden people if I speak about it, but if you don't talk about it, then it will only get worse.

I'm thankful to know the people that I do you give me such an incredible support.

This book you are reading will help you understand that you are not alone and you are so loved.

Always remember, life is what you make it.

Joseph x

Kevin

An old man was talking to a boy and said. "There are two wolves always fighting inside me. One is filled with anger, hate, jealousy, shame and lies. The other wolf is filled with love, joy, truth and peace. This battle rages inside of you and all men." The boy thought for a moment and asked, "Which wolf will win?" The old man answered, "The one you feed."

We stood in the cold under the floodlit sign that warns people to 'chain up' right where the mountain highway and the logging road meet. The logging road was taped off with police denying access and clearly some activity close by. The tracker on our daughter's phone led us to that spot. Her roommates were already there, equally anxious. We were kept in the dark for several hours, eventually, back at the police stations, we met with the coroner who asked us to give details of Coco's tattoos and piercings. She had a new tattoo, 'I hope you dance' on her side as a gift to me for Father's Day. As the dreaded words were spoken, I sat focused on my wife as I watched in shock as the joy leave her body and the agony come pouring out.

My name is Kevin, and it's been 18 months and eight days since we lost our daughter. I'm not a writer, just a dad who has lost the most precious gift in the world. I will do my best to share how we have been affected.

The memories of the night Coco died will never leave me. It was the worst day of our lives. Mothers intuition was on a high and had been on a high for over a year, since her first shocking attempt at taking her life. Mom's intuition saved her that morning. It came shortly after a particular bout of Mononucleosis. The jokes about it being the 'kissing disease stopped.

Courtney (Coco) was 22, and she was the light of our lives. When that light extinguished, our world was plunged into darkness. If you are Irish, you will understand this line, Coco was "the fizz in my Tanora, without her life gets flat." (Tanora is a soft drink).

If Coco had entered your world in any way, I am positive she has touched your heart.

You may think these are the words of a very proud dad but believe me when I tell you she was the happiest of souls. When I would return from a business trip, as I came in the front door, I would listen for the sound of her sprinting across the hardwood floor and waited for the spider monkey embrace as she launched herself at me with pure joy and love.

In the psychiatric hospital, she picked up some bad habits. She started self-harming. Coco posted the following on social media. "I can only take so much pain until my body is slowly overflowing with hurtful words and repressed memories". After treatment, Coco struggled with depression, and again her social media gives a glimpse into her mind. "I want to give up. I'm done with myself, but no matter how depressed I am, no matter how much it's killing me, I can't leave because I care too much. I know this would destroy my family, so I take this pain. I've chosen to smile although I'm dying inside in the hope that the people, I love don't get depressed."

Coco worked hard to beat depression. We truly believed she had finally found inner peace, we spent quality time together over her last few weeks, and she was happy and loving.

For mom, the worry was a constant companion. Occasionally a post would invite mild anxiety. One such post haunts me, "I'm the girl that talks others out of suicide, but has a hard time doing the same for herself. She truthfully assures everyone how beautiful, lovely, wonderful and precious they all are because she doesn't want them to feel like she does; the opposite."

Immediately after Coco's death, we were in a fog. Friends, family, the entire community cradled us, supported us through the rollercoaster of grief. I cried so hard I thought my heart would burst out of my chest, my lungs screaming for air, my brain on fire. I had by now been off work for nearly two years with a serious heart condition. I was grateful for the opportunity to spend so much time at home and had hoped being present was helping Coco's recovery. My cardiologist called to advise me how damaging grief can be on my much-compromised heart. I took to keeping a diary when I needed to share my thoughts and calm my inner monsters privately.

March 19, 2019: "I'm so sad I wish I was dead." I secretly hoped my heart condition would give me a guilt-free escape.

It was challenging to find counselling for survivors of suicide. Our first attempt at sharing our story left the professional sobbing in her chair.

In an effort to organize my thoughts and feelings, and in response to the lack of resources available, I started making the following list.

A SURVIVOR'S GUIDE TO SUICIDE (WORK IN PROGRESS).

1. **BREATHE**: Research breathing techniques, and it honestly calms the mind and body. Simply put, this action saved my life.

2. **WHY**: A permanent solution to a temporary problem. Why the Instagram post simply tagged, "Atelphobia". Why on the mountain?

3. **GUILT**: Is a monster. Be vigilant; don't let it get hold of you. The 'should have could have' thoughts are persistent. Self-talk and rationalization are key to maintaining sanity. I've had to accept the fact that I cannot change the past and learn to live in a new reality.

4. **ANGER**: Can be described as the lazy emotion. In the beginning, I wanted to assign blame. There are people who I believe selfishly contributed to my daughter's state of mind. I wanted to put my HULK suit on and smash. The story of the two wolves at the opening truly gives me perspective every day. I and only I have the power to feed the wolves. The choice is mine. I choose to feed the happy wolf.

5. **GRIEF**: Buckle up, it will hit you often, especially when you least expect it. Sometimes it feels like a light shower, sometimes a tsunami. It knows no boundaries. We felt desperately alone, even in a crowded room of loved ones. A new counsellor who specialized in grief had just moved to town, we found her at a local hospice. When she asked (after several sessions) what I hoped to get out of these appointments, I thought about it long and hard. I realized I just wished to know I was not losing my mind. I learned strategies on how to deal with my emotions. My wife needed a deeper level of therapy, EMDR. It's a process;

we see and feel improvement. It's important to find a professional to talk to. Don't be stubborn; get help. I would like to note here that we have not hesitated to reach out to others in our community who have suffered a similar loss. Sharing the grief does help lighten the burden.

6. **PAIN**: The physical pain is real. A broken heart actually feels like your heart is broken. Breathing exercises help.

7. **FRIENDS**: Let them help you. Witnessing my wife's grief is crippling. Our close friends 'carried' us through the days and weeks we were unable to function. I'm eternally grateful to them all for their love and support. Friends often came to visit, and some would be hysterically crying in our home. This had to stop. Boundaries had to be set. Mindful of their grief made this a difficult message to deliver at an emotionally charged time. I used the analogy that grief was like a 500-pound backpack. I was doing my best to carry mine and my wife's. 'I cannot carry yours too.' If you are coming to visit us, come and help with this enormous weight. Please don't add to it. Stay away. Send a text with a heart emoji instead. Every little bit helps.

8. **The ripple effect:** We became acutely aware of Coco's friends who were suffering from mental health issues. A neighbour and friend of Coco's took his life at home a short five months later. His dad shared with me that "anxiety and worry had been replaced with a heavy sadness"—two other families in our circle who have suffered similar losses in the past year. We are in club none of us ever wanted to join.

It's OK to cry.

It's OK to laugh.

It's OK to take a nap and have some alone time.

It's OK not to feel OK.

It's OK to turn your phone off and breathe.

For those who may read this and know, truly know, you are having negative thoughts or mental health issues. Please pause; Breathe; Ask for help; Set small goals, celebrate small victories. Recognize the danger signs. This world really is a much better place with you in it even if you can't see that right now.

One blessing I hold close to my heart is my little niece Erin. She has silenced the sceptic in me regarding an afterlife. Several people have come to us with stories of dreams, visions and mes-sages from beyond. HOWEVER, the pure innocence of Erin and the messages she delivers leave me no doubt that our daughter soul lives on. I believe she is with us. We are just not evolved enough to see, hear or understand what waits beyond this world.

Take a moment to smile at everyone you meet. You never know, you could save a life today.

Kimberly

My name is Kimberly – I am 30 now, and I was 22 and 26 when I attempted suicide.

The first time, I was kind of manic. I had been off work for a long time and was due back on Monday. I was on medication and started to feel a little more under control. I agreed to meet up with colleagues from work on Friday night, so I could catch up with people, hoping it would make me feel less nervous about coming back.

They were awful to me. I don't think they even knew how hard their words hit. But on my way home, I was drunk and upset. I then tried to take my own life.

I knew at the time I had not taken enough – but I felt so desperate for someone to know just how bad I felt.

The second time – I consider a serious attempt. I planned it. I knew I didn't want to keep on living if this would be my life. 'This' being long-standing, severe depression. It was preventing me from being myself and preventing me from having meaningful relationships, jobs, hobbies, health.

I couldn't see any other way out. I didn't want to die, but I didn't want to live.

I planned the day – I took a bath; I changed into clean pyjamas and took myself to my bedroom. I felt like I wanted to be clean and comfortable.

I took an overdose, then as soon as I stopped being to keep my eyes open, I laid in bed.

I wanted to fall asleep and never wake up.

But I did – and then a barrage of questions came. 'Why have you done this?' 'What are you playing at?' 'Why didn't you talk to us?'.

You don't expect to have to answer these questions.

The person in the hospital next to me I'll never forget her. She was crying out in pain, and I believe she had cancer. I felt guilty. I felt guilty that I had put myself here and needed these nurses to help me when there were people in here who probably would have wished to switch bodies with me. I remember thinking then for the first time in years; I could choose to stay alive.

HOW ARE YOU NOW?

I now consider myself to be 'recovered' – in that I can manage myself, recognise symptoms, speak openly and understand my feelings.

WHAT YOU FEEL NEEDS TO CHANGE?

Social attitudes toward depression and anxiety need to change. I feel there has been a shift in society – it's okay now more than ever to speak about it – but what then? People still freeze up, people still refer you to someone else, hospitals and doctors are still overwhelmed, and their 'go-to' is a packet of tablets. I feel that if society as a whole felt able to talk about emotions, talk about how they feel, what they need, what needs to change in their lives – so many of us wouldn't' t get to 'crises'.

WHAT HELPED YOU?

I feel strongly that choosing to stay alive helped me the most. I was then able to accept the help I would need to do that. Counselling was the most incredible journey I have ever been on, and I still attend today. Counselling has changed my relationship with myself and how I view others. It's taught me how to handle certain feelings and emotions – as well as how to challenge perceptions.

WHAT DIDN'T HELP YOU?

I would say it's the social attitudes, especially back when I was suffering the most. My employers, family and friends didn't understand and didn't want to. It made the journey so much more isolating – it made me feel like I was abnormal.

THE BEST ADVICE YOU CAN GIVE SOMEONE GOING THROUGH YOUR TRAUMA.

Seeking help for your trauma supports you to get back in touch with that 'gut feeling' that you've lost by covering yourself up for so long. You lose it by pretending to be someone you're not for someone else's comfort.

Once you have that feeling back – it's the only tool you'll ever need to keep yourself safe and well.

Marie

"I was a sex worker in the Whitechapel East London area for some time, because ironically I didn't want to 'work' the streets in my local area, mostly down to a fear of somebody I knew to see me. It was at this time that the Ipswich strangler was killing his victims. I remember the news being flooded with images of these women, warnings for sex workers in Ipswich and the surrounding areas not to go out onto the streets, and the police presence in Whitechapel being stepped up. The police would get out of the car, ask if we were 'ok' and warn us about what was happening to these poor girls in the Ipswich area.

DID THIS STOP ME GOING OUT ON DARK NIGHTS?

No, it didn't.

WAS I SCARED?

I was absolutely petrified.

Then why couldn't I stop? The answer is I had totally lost all of my power to heroin and crack cocaine. I started taking crack and heroin at the very tender age of 17, not aware of the dangers or effects this was about to have on me, or my children's devastating lives and I still live with them today. Even after being in abstinent based recovery for over four years I still live with the effects of my sex work, the harms I caused to myself have left me with deep-rooted pain and trauma, and I live with complex PTSD. I live with nightmares, triggers, and sadness for the young girl I lost to the men I gave myself to so cheaply."

Of course, dealing with all of these issues isn't easy. Multiple drug addictions, PTSD, nightmares, depression – all of these things are a challenge to recover from alone, so dealing with all of them is understandably one of the most challenging experiences a person can go through.

"After coming into recovery, I wasn't even aware of the effects my sex work had on me. I was walking around consistently angry, the nightmares I was having also were having a huge impact, but I just put that down to coming out of my addiction. I couldn't manage or maintain friendships or my relationship. I just put that down to defects of character.

As I went further along in my recovery, my mental health was deteriorating, anxiety, panic, fear and a feeling of constant dread, I wasn't making the connection. Nobody in meetings could diagnose me. My support network wasn't able to do anything; I was actively pushing my friends away daily. Nobody was allowed to hug me or make physical contact. Even if my sponsor went to touch my shoulder, I would cringe inside. I was in pain. Deep-rooted trauma caused by my actions to feed my addiction, and I wasn't even aware of this at the time."

It turns out what got this person on the road to recovery was a chance meeting with the right person:

"Within all of this, someone saw me. Chip Somers from Private Practice London kindly reached out to me and offered me some free Skype counselling. I had had therapy before, but that was when I was still using drugs, and consequently, I was never open or honest, and a result, nothing ever worked. I gave him my background – my mother also suffers from the disease of addiction, my father had left when I was four, and I was rejected daily by Mum because all she cared about was using drugs.

I see this today as neglect and mental abuse on a child. Hugs or physical affection were not a common thing in our house. Different men were coming into the home, and sexual and physical abuse took place there regularly.

I briefly touched on my sex work in the session. Chip was very good with me. He made me feel safe and supported me throughout the process. At the end of my session, Chip started to guide me to areas that I needed to work on.

I was stunned by his statement" You need to look at your sex work, Marie".

I responded, "I'm ok now, I was powerless. I know why I did it."

Little did I know that by saying this, my mind was shutting out the trauma from it.

I will never forget what he said next:

"Don't be so bloody surprised Marie, your sex work is affecting every area of your life, and there is a link to your past trauma that made you be able to go and fund your habit that way".

"Don't be so bloody surprised Marie, your sex work is affecting every area of your life, and there is a link to your past trauma that made you be able to go and fund your habit that way".

I was stunned. Every part of my being didn't want to believe him; I had always thought the link to my troubles was down to my parents and my upbringing. I do not blame or justify my using on my past anymore; I take full responsibility for it. I've made some very poor choices regarding drug use, and there have been devastating consequences not just to me, but to others. Nothing has caused me more harm than my sex work.

I'm incredibly grateful to Chip and his support; I feel if it wasn't identified when it was, the guilt, shame and anger I was carrying around would have eventually taken me back to a relapse at some point.

Since that session with Chip, I have completed the 12 steps and looked at my sex work throughout the process. I added myself to my amends list as part of the process. The Step four process was challenging for me at times – the sexual inventory and abuse section raised my memories and issues to the surface.

I was 15 months clean and writing around an issue I had no awareness of myself. It felt dangerous to my mental health and my recovery to unearth this stuff so early as I had huge amounts of internal shame linked to the sex work that I had been hiding from myself.

The anger I felt was towards myself!

For years, I thought I was simply angry at the world.

I remember heading out to the local 'red-light' area for the first time like it was yesterday. I can remember thinking to myself "well he's taken it all from me anyway". I was thinking about my abuser as a child.

I don't remember my first punter. I don't remember my last, I don't remember cars or names, but I remember men, lots of men and I remember their smell.

The winter months were horrendous. I've spent weeks of dark, cold nights standing out there hour after hour, the temperature below freezing and my withdrawals from heroin biting my skin and bones. Tears streaming down my face because I just want to go home, but I don't, I can't, I need my next fix more than anything else could ever matter, even my health and safety.

The summer months were not much help either, it got dark later, so less money was earned, and police more commonly patrolled the red-light area, so my convictions were clocking up with time.

There is nothing more embarrassing than having to stand in a magistrate's court charged with soliciting. Talking about the matter in police interviews wasn't much fun either. Being locked up for nearly 24 hours in withdrawal is really not the way to help a person who is clearly extremely vulnerable and damaged! Not once in my process of court orders was, I offered counselling or help around my sex work. No helped was ever offered to me on any of these occasions.

Instead, they would just lock me up until my withdrawal symptoms got completely unbearable, then drop me back off where they found me, enforcing the cycle if anything.

I had a terrible experience out there one night. A man had picked me up while I was going through major withdrawal, and I wasn't able to do what he was asking from me.

As a result, I was raped.

I was held at my throat and forced into doing a sexual act I didn't want to do.

After he was finished with me, I didn't go to the police, and I didn't go home. I returned directly to the red-light area, as I still needed the money for my next fix.

It may sound crazy, but this is the hold drugs had over me, and thousands of women on our streets right now.

I experienced a total loss of control. I was sore and utterly numb to what had just happened to me. And this is how my life continued for 15 years, in and out of punters cars and at some points working in brothels. In the brothels, my addiction would go through the roof as the people running these places were mainly coke dealers and would give me free tasters to keep me there.

Not once was I aware of the damage I was causing myself.

Since coming into recovery in June 2014, it has been tough. Living with the Complex PTSD caused by my experiences has been one of the hardest battles I've had to deal with. My symptoms are feelings of anger, fear, dread, irritability, restlessness, discontent. On a bad day, I feel like I'm going to stop breathing, I get hyper-vigilant, have sleep paralysis, flashbacks and night terrors.

I isolate myself in an attempt to keep myself safe from the outside world. Today, I have an awareness of what is happening, and I know my triggers. I've learnt about my mental health by reading books and looking it up on the internet. I connect with other addicts who can talk honestly with me and who I trust. I feel it's really important when talking about my symptoms to find the right people, people who can just listen, not advise, and just let me be and people who don't make the situation about them and dismiss my feelings.

While the 12 steps are a great tool, some things they just cannot fix. The steps are like the wind at the top of a volcano, blowing away all the lava and dust and keeping me alive, but under all that is the fire that is bubbling away under the surface. I would never have been able to get rid of that without outside help.

I've been in therapy for just over a year now. I get close to the core of the problem then stop because it gets that painful, but I keep going back.

I will heal, I am improving every day I don't pick up drugs, I'm healing in one form or another from my trauma always. I'm most definitely not a victim of my past, and I take responsibility for the harms I have caused to myself. I've become a survivor, and I refuse to let my addiction or mental health issues define me as a person. I'm a mum today, a sponsor, a sponsee, a friend and employee, an active member of the fellowship I attend.

What I'm incredibly grateful for is that I'm no longer a sex worker, a 'working girl', a prostitute. I'm me, a recovering addict free from the seedy streets, cars, and punters. When it's dark and raining, and I'm inside, an immense feeling of gratitude comes over me. I will never forget the street corners I stood on, the cars, or smells, but what I will always remember is how lucky I am that I've gained control of my life. By healing and facing my trauma head-on, I will never have to subject myself to such pain and hurt again."

However, Marie goes on to explain that the sex industry doesn't only hurt sex workers:

"I feel I would also like to add how some of my 'clients' became my victims. There were some very vulnerable, lonely men out there, often with their own mental health problems and addiction troubles.

Me being the very manipulative addict that I was, could spot these issues from a mile away and knew exactly how to let it benefit me.

I had one client remortgage his house to fund my addiction, and he cleared any savings out of his account that he had. I've had other men who know absolutely nothing about addiction take me to houses to score drugs at 2 am.

I've shouted at them, I've screamed at them when I think I can get away with it, I've stolen car keys, house keys and I've also taken the money and run. This is known in the streets as clipping.

There was more often than not a retaliation. I've been beaten up and attacked several occasions by the men I've stolen from, but that won't stop you when you need the money for drugs.

Sex work doesn't just affect the person selling themselves. Married men get found out, destroying marriages. Neighbours have to contend with strange men kerb-crawling around their streets at night, and having the girls walking up and down, making a noise. Condoms, needles and drug paraphernalia are often left lying around for people to have to pick up in the morning. It affects everybody in the area."

My experiences are profound, real, and horrifying.

But one thing they aren't is unique.

There are people all across the UK and the world going through similar experiences right now. You might even be one of them yourself, or maybe a loved one is.

Mark

My name is Mark. I'm 58 years old. I have struggled with addictions and mental health for the past six years.

I was born into a working-class south London background. My dad left when I was six months old, and I've never seen him since. My mum was 17 at the time, but my childhood was a very happy one, albeit being an only child, it was quite lonely at times. I always wanted to be a soldier and joined when I was 19. I spent eight years travelling the world, including three tours in Northern Ireland. I was married and had a baby son but left all that behind when I met someone else, she didn't follow me into civvie street, but I carried on.

My civvie life was hard at first, but I got a good job at Gatwick Airport and worked there for 30 years. I was married two more times, but neither worked out, which sadly were my fault. After my last marriage broke down, I had a mental breakdown, which didn't help with having 3months off work. I was then diagnosed with stress and possibly PTSD, and on top of this, I was drinking uncontrollably. The NHS wouldn't help with intervention because of my drinking, so I tried to take my life twice, but thankfully I wasn't sectioned.

I was put onto citalopram 10mg a day and received some counselling; however, my anger began to manifest itself in other ways. I was arrested twice for assault and public order, although I have no recollection of what I did, my life was out of control.

I then started meeting other women through dating sites and was introduced to drugs and sex parties, more bad life choices, soon I was regularly taking MDMA and cocaine, and still drinking hard, while holding down a regular job. Something had to give and what gave was me. I had another breakdown; I couldn't cope and started to feel paranoid. One night at a party they had to call an Ambulance because they thought I was having some sort of stroke, I wasn't thanking god, but it was a wake-up call.

I've now been drug-free for four months. I feel better for it. However, I still drink and can go on 2 to 3-day benders, depending on my mental state, when I drink, I can be a deceitful and manipulative individual. Yet, strangely a popular person in the pub, a tissue of lies beneath a veneer to be desperately valued and liked, and no counsellor I've been to can work that one out.

I've been going to the LRF men's group since December, and to be honest, it has helped me tremendously, a safe non-judgmental space for us all to talk openly about our problems, I hold back a few things as I don't think it's fair to hog all the time allowed, but it helps, it helps a lot.

I've now started a new job driving for Tesco's which means I have to curb my drinking, but that is an everyday battle, shadow boxing I call it dodging punches sometimes you can, and sometimes you take on crack on the jaw.

The woman at the start of my story who didn't follow me into civvie street, well she has been with me the past two years, and she tries her level best to help me, I go to church a few times a month light a candle and say the serenity prayer, sounds weird but it helps.

I want to try more counselling, but I am wary of them to be truthful, so going forward it's about trying to find the inner strength to find inner peace and be comfortable with who and what I am.

Nicola

I have been called strong, brave, inspirational so many times I have almost come to rely on the words as a coping mechanism. But how do we decide someone is strong and brave, is it because I try not to complain or show my fear, but instead strive for normality through my fight against secondary breast cancer. For a long time, I thought to be brave was saying 'I'm fine' or smiling through my pain, so much so, that even when I allowed myself to accept the offer of counselling, I was too embarrassed to tell anyone. So, I lied about where I was going and made excuses so that people wouldn't have to know that I was weak, and not this brave, inspirational person they once thought I was.

For as long as I can remember, I have been an anxious person; this was only heightened by the loss of my mum to ovarian cancer when I was in my late teens. I was a shy teenager and like most girls relied on my mum for friendship, comfort and encouragement, I loved nothing more than jumping into her bed on a Sunday morning so I could fill her in on all the antics of the Saturday night before. Losing her was like having my safety net snatched away, not only was I terrified about how I would cope without her, but I also put an enormous amount of pressure on myself to become self-supporting, make her proud, and take care of the family. I guess in a sense I tried to step into her shoes and in some small way, make up for the loss I knew everyone was feeling. I focused on everyone else's pain so I could bury my own.

Over time I developed an ability to completely detach myself from my emotions, a skill that got me through treatment for my primary diagnosis of Breast cancer but was in no way beneficial to my mental health. I was just 25 when I received my breast cancer diagnosis and underwent a mastectomy, chemotherapy and radiotherapy, all while trying to reduce the impact on the people I love, I often played down how I was feeling so not to burden anyone, and for a long time this worked well for me, it made it easier for me to pretend everything was normal. As soon as my radiotherapy was complete, I threw myself back into Uni, bought our first house, got married to my fiancé, who had proposed just two months before my diagnosis. We then started planning for a baby which meant taking a break from the Tamoxifen, hormone treatment I was on. It was as if I was suddenly in a rush to achieve all the things I had hoped for in life, while I had the chance before cancer reared its ugly head again, it was just one achievement after another, never giving myself time to reflect on what I had been through.

Sadly, my first pregnancy ended in a missed miscarriage; three years had passed since the day I was told chemotherapy would likely render me infertile, so you can imagine how excited I was about my 12-week scan, I was finally going to see my baby, finally have more proof than a stick I had peed on that I was going to be a mummy. Still, instead, I suddenly found myself being referred for surgery to remove the 'products of conception' My dreams shattered I couldn't figure out why? How could this happen? Hadn't I been through enough already? I was sure this was a sign I would never gain the title of a mummy. I was in a deep dark hole, and I wondered if I would ever be able to drag myself back out, I'd faced so much with a positive front, but this almost completely broke me. My saviour was a beautiful little puppy, called Rowan, of course getting her in no way replaced the baby I had lost, a sadness I still feel to this day, but she gave me a focus, an outlet for all the love I had wanted to share with my baby, a reason to move forward. I did go on to have two further successful pregnancies and could not be more grateful for my amazing children, Dylan and Poppy.

But being a Mummy only intensified my anxiety, I have always struggled with the smaller stuff, but suddenly this became worse, things that may seem trivial to others are at times impossible for me to overcome. I am a terribly anxious driver, sticking to routes I know, and not using motorways; I have sometimes avoided social situations because I get so anxious about how I will make it home safely, I worry about how people perceive me, not living up to expectation, every small noise or bump in the night fills me with dread, even mildly adverse weather could send me into a state of panic. I have developed the ability to catastrophise even the smallest of troubles.

It wasn't until my secondary breast cancer diagnosis at the age of 34 that I began to see these completely irrational fears for what they were. I attended six counselling sessions on the premise that I may struggle with the hormone imbalance of going from 4 months Postpartum to the medically induced menopause that my treatment required. Still, deep down, I knew that wasn't the only reason I needed to give counselling a try. It didn't take long for the therapist I saw to figure me out either, she seemed particularly surprised at the way I had described my situation, 'flat', 'without emotion' was the words I believe she used. I was reluctantly forced to dig deep during the six sessions, and there wasn't a day that I left her office without feeling a little overwhelmed with emotion, a feeling that had become somewhat alien to me. She helped me to see that mentally I had been working so hard to keep all of my feelings suppressed that small things that may seem irrelevant to many were enough to make me feel like I had lost control. I also discovered that I had become so concerned with convincing everyone I was able to cope that I had not only lost the ability to ask for help, but also to accept help when its offered. I tried several different CBT techniques during my counselling sessions but found the time was more productive to air my feelings and share the pain I had buried with someone completely impartial. Someone who wouldn't feel burdened by my confessions of fear, wouldn't judge me for struggling with my emotions, someone that could listen and encourage me to be honest with myself.

The counselling was so beneficial in helping me face the fears that I had suppressed for so long. However, I still felt overwhelmed by the anxiety I was feeling in certain situations, so I began taking prescribed medication, which was under the advice of the GP, to help me get back in control. I still feel anxiety and fear but am more equipped now to rationalise and try to overcome it. I worry about where I would be now if I hadn't finally plucked up the courage to admit I needed some help. For me, true bravery and strength lie in being able to face your truth, be honest with yourself and accept that sometimes it's ok to need a bit of help, something I am still learning to do.

Rhiannon

My story on postnatal depression.

I grew up in a family of four with me being the youngest; I have an older brother who I am incredibly close with. It was a middle-class family home, and my mum and dad were extremely hard working and always made sure that my brother and I didn't go without. I always struggled with anxiety as I was growing up, but it was controlled, and I only had times that I found it hard to manage when I was starting something new or an exam that I had to prepare for. I then went to the Brit school of performing arts, where I found myself and had some of the best years of my life. Everyone had their dreams when they were in school, a dancer, footballer, singer, actress etc. My dream was to be a mum, I had always loved children, and as I grew older, I began to volunteer for children with learning disabilities at the YMCA. Before I knew it, I was 23 and pregnant with my first child. I was quite anxious throughout my pregnancy because I wanted my little boy so badly and was convinced it was too good to be true, and as the pregnancy continued the hormones and fatigue only increased that anxiety.

My labour was anything but straightforward, and I was in labour for 36 hours, and my baby was back to back, which means he was facing the wrong way. It ended up being a forceps delivery but as soon as he was put on my chest, and the emergency doctors had left the room, it was love at first sight. I remember not being able to take my eyes off him.

As the first week passed my worry that something was going to happen to him wouldn't shift, and it only got worse as time went on. I cried every single day, and at night I could barely sleep even when the baby slept, all because of the fear that something terrible was going to happen. Family members would want to cuddle him and feed him, and it made me feel extremely uncomfortable. That fear also meant that I refused to allow myself to bond with him because I was convinced the love I felt for him was going to be taken away from me. I was in A&E every week pleading with the doctors to look at him, wanting every test because I was so sure he was unwell. The doctors tried to be reassuring, but it wasn't enough, and I was confident they were missing something, I didn't trust them and nothing anyone said to me made me believe that everything was in fact okay. I felt angry that I wasn't being listened to by anyone. I stopped talking to people and every day seemed to merge into one, I was jumpy, paranoid and extremely emotional.

One day my friend took him out to visit some family so I could rest, I woke up and stood up and went to get him out of the cot which was always the usual routine after nap time. I still; to this day, vividly remember placing him on the bed, and then I blinked, and he was gone. I searched for him and panicked, I couldn't' t hear him breathing anymore, and I couldn't' t see him, I remember screaming for him and crying. I was convinced he was trapped somewhere, and the longer time went on, my panic grew into a full-blown panic attack. In the process of ripping the bed and room apart, my friend called, and I answered, sobbing down the phone while I explained. My friend then reminded me that they had him and they were with family. I was so confused because what I had just experienced had felt so real, I went downstairs and ran myself a bath and sat in it numbly, it was then I realised, I needed help.

I went to the doctors who referred me to the mother and infant mental health team; there I was diagnosed with postnatal depression and traits of psychosis. I had suffered hallucinations, intrusive thoughts of harming myself, and it scares me to think what it would have developed into if I had not received help when I did. Fatigue plays a massive part in the deterioration of mental health. Although having a newborn meant that to the extent that couldn't be helped, I was under strict orders that I was to sleep at every opportunity. I was prescribed antidepressants and anti-psychotics and given one on one sessions with a psychologist. Although the medications helped until it got to the 4-month mark and the risk of cot death lessened it was only then that my anxiety started to lift, and I believed that my baby was here to stay. I still suffer from anxiety and depression now, I still take antidepressants and a suppressant for my anxiety, but through extensive counselling, I was able to bond with my second baby a lot easier and didn't suffer from the postnatal stress as I did with my first. The fear in my second pregnancy was nowhere near as bad, and for that reason, I was able to enjoy it more. Although bonding with my second baby was a lot easier, my mental health once again deteriorated, and I was closely monitored in case I suffered any more hallucinations. I was overwhelmed when my second baby arrived and did find it hard to cope but slowly over time, with support from my family, the breathing techniques and knowledge I had been taught I was able to rationalise the panic and kept my head above water.

I hope that in the future to have more children and to enjoy the experience in full. I have a wonderful partner and two lovely little boys, and for that, I couldn't be more thankful. Sometimes I look at the boys and my home and realise how far I have come. I love being able to take them out and spend one on one time with them both. Although the terrible twos are in full swing and my eldest is a teenager, I wouldn't' t change the chaos for the world, and I am so proud of myself for battling through some of the toughest days I have ever experienced and made it to where I am today. I am excited to see them grow and nurture them through life. I will always make sure they are informed about mental health and to know never to be ashamed of speaking out if they find themselves struggling.

My advice to anyone that thinks they are suffering or may know someone suffering from postnatal depression or psychosis is to speak out. The embarrassment I felt that I was doing something wrong and for fear of being judged, meant I put myself, my mental health and potentially my baby at a massive risk. If I could go back and speak out sooner, I would have because the illness robbed me of some of the most beautiful first days with my baby. Please remember, it is not your fault, you are not doing anything wrong, and people can help you. You never have to battle in silence and every day is a new day with the potential of a better life.

Sylvia

The home is where the heart is, but what if nowhere felt like home? I was born and raised in Auckland, New Zealand with an Indonesian mother and Kiwi father. I vividly remember the utopia that we resided in for the first 12 years of my life; my Norfolk pine treehouse that made me feel like I was in an alternate universe, fruit and vegetables in abundance, a horse paddock over the fence and a garage roof that I often climbed atop to perform pop songs to my neighbours. Much of my spare time was spent caring for animals, observing the metamorphosis of the caterpillars to chrysalides to Monarch butterflies, getting the horses to chase after me for an adrenaline kick and dabbling in the odd PS1 game. Although my memory of childhood is somewhat limited, I do recall my parents being indefatigable in their pursuit to create a beautiful life for my brother and me.

I remember being fiercely independent - started paid employment at the age of eight as a paper runner and have not been without work since then. I wanted to buy my own schoolbooks and uniform in a bid to relieve my parents of financial stress, as I had heard them argue about finances a few times. I was a charismatic, compassionate, hard-working, intelligent and an athletic little girl that had everything going for her. Until everything collapsed in front of me and I went through adversities that no one should ever have to endure.

My first memorable trauma was witnessing my feathered companion decapitated and later served as dinner. Like a mirror thrown off a three-storey building, I felt my stomach drop, and my heart shatter into a thousand irreparable pieces. Unable to contain my sorrow, the empath in me contemplated my friend's short existence. To have my life shortened, no matter what conditions I am subjected to, in order to satisfy the taste buds of humankind. From that point onwards, I refused to eat meat, which didn't go down particularly well with a father who grew up on farms. I wouldn't be allowed to leave the dinner table until I finished my meal in its entirety, so I would fall asleep in protest. I am still the same animal-loving, defender of the voiceless that I was when I was eight.

When I was nine years old, I experienced my next significant trauma(s) which subsequently affected me for two decades. In the dead of night, I was in sweet slumber, drifting into dreamland before being lost in oblivion. Dazed, perplexed and full of fear, I opened my eyelids to discover a head stationed in between my legs. I lay there frozen, unable to move even a muscle fibre at the thought of escape. The touch was unfamiliar, but the person was all too familiar. My first cousin who was married with children would spit out vile words to tear me down by day and by night would play Freddy from A Nightmare on Elm Street, capitalising on any opportunity to haunt and slowly kill me. Sometimes it would feel like I was being stabbed by sharp blades. The sexual abuse and rape continued for seven years, despite having told a few people when I was 12. I desperately wanted someone to rescue me, to remove me from this toxic environment that was supposedly my home. Betrayed by those who I thought I could confide in; I saw no hope in the near or distant future.

No one was there to protect me, no one heard my cries, and even when I spoke, I was not heard. I felt invisible and condemned to a life of loneliness.

Life was relentless with the number of curveballs it consistently threw at me. But I was proactive in my endeavour to give life's terrors and terrible people the middle finger, starting my journey of martial arts when I was ten years old. I took up Karate at school then went on to Taekwondo before finding Muay Thai and Brazilian Jiu-Jitsu. Martial arts gave me direction, discipline and the confidence to sometimes stand up for myself. The home was unsafe, but so was school. The abuse had, in turn, made me hypersexual, so I started experimenting from a disturbingly young age, and word got around. From about 11 years old, I was coined a "slut" until the end of my school days. Fed up with being bullied, I got into some pretty wild fights to stand up for myself. Although I was a head down, arse up goodie-two-shoes that had never once had a detention, I was nearly suspended for beating up three boys in assembly. I hated school almost as much as I hated myself.

Sex and love became one and the same for me – an entanglement of deceit, dirtiness and some validation. I developed OCD with cleaning because of how dirty how I felt inside and out. My seemingly conspicuous vulnerability increased my susceptibility to victimisation by several other men. I was violently raped when I was 11 years old by two men at a local park while going for an evening run. And anally raped by a boy I fancied when I was 12. I have been raped more times than I can count, and for many years I blamed myself. When I looked into the mirror, all I saw was ugliness, and all I felt was repulsion. It was like a horror movie inside my head, and I was imprisoned in this cell with hysteria. I cried myself to sleep almost every night for as long as I can remember.

When I was 14 years old, I got into a relationship with someone who initially treated me the way the princesses were treated in fairy tales. He looked at me as if I was the only person that mattered. Romanced me with roses and words from the heart, spoken with immense passion. I felt held, I felt loved; I felt all my suffering dissolve for a moment. Six months into the relationship, the switch was tampered with and what stood before me was a complete stranger. This person who I thought I loved started to display intense jealousy, forcing me to stop friendships with all males. He controlled how I spent my time and how I dressed. If I disobeyed his orders, I would receive verbal abuse followed by a beating. My body was often dressed in bruises and open wounds. There were times where I found my feet and would fight back, which would often result in an even greater beating. One particularly memorable time was when he found out I was still in contact with one of my male friends. He scalped my head and smashed it on the wooden floor a few times before soccer kicking my ribs.

I was knocked out cold. Interestingly, none of my family and friends ever suspected a thing, even during the times I was hobbling around with a limp. This sadist who I thought at one point was an amazing boyfriend, took great pleasure in tearing me down.

Consistently telling me that I'm worthless and that I'm lucky he's with me considering how "dirty" I am. I believed him and became dependant on him for validation. He was as much a curse as my cousin was, and I felt my whole world ripped beneath my feet once again. While we were still together, he had an arranged marriage, and I never saw him again. One thing that I am grateful for is that he is the one person to finally stand up to my cousin and stopped the abuse from ever happening again.

Dancing between the feelings of self-hatred and complete emptiness, I took to self-mutilation to distract me from the stinging stabs of emotional pain. I butchered my body but concealed it so well, again no one suspected a thing. Or if they did, they sure as shit didn't say anything. I contemplated a more permanent solution to ending my torment.

What ultimately gave me purpose and saved my life back then was finding something beyond myself to care for. My father collapsed in front of me when I was 12 or 13 – had a stroke and was diagnosed with Parkinson's Disease. Caring for him and my animal babies became my top priorities. I cared for him until he tripped over and hit his head against the corner of a desk, which caused brain haemorrhaging beyond repair. He slipped into a coma and died just a few days after my wedding.

My life has had no shortage of adversities, traumas and loss of loved ones, but still, I stand here alive and kicking. I have experienced tempestuous times that have knocked the wind out of me and made me question my existence. How did I cope? As a child, I quickly learnt the art of acting – my coping mechanism was concealing all my pain behind a smiling mask. Many would call me a beacon of positivity or the life of the party, without a clue of the darkness that I had become rather intimate with. My world started falling apart when I was nine, but I was clinically diagnosed with depression and PTSD when I was 14.

What made those childhood and teenage years survivable was being heavily distracted with work, school, volunteering, sports and caring for loved ones. I was not at an age where I could fully comprehend what was going on underneath the surface. Having a creative outlet to express my feelings was helpful, and I did this mainly in the form of poetry. When I put pen to paper, I felt surges of what it felt like to be free and unapologetically write exactly what I was feeling. My turbulent emotions had the opportunity of both swimming with and against the current in a dramatic yet divine dance with darkness.

The dance with darkness will forever be portrayed in the scars I wear. They serve as a painful reminder of the many battles faced, but I am not ashamed of them. Suicidal thoughts were ever-present, and attempts were made to end my pestilent misery. Being the survivor that I am, I managed to pull through and come out the other side. My near fatal actions were not without consequences. They affected my relationships, my interactions with people and caused a whole lot of internal chaos for a long while. If I could turn back the clock...

My quest to find inner tranquillity became more apparent with each year that I grew wiser. I struggled with my identity and my purpose. Who the fuck am I? Why do bad things always happen to me? Desperate to find something to calm the treacherous storms, I read up on the law of attraction and adopted a genuinely optimistic attitude. The keyword here is genuine - I spent much of life emitting a positive energy that wasn't felt in the core of my being and this resulted in energy vampirism (having the life sucked out of me). Phenomenal things can happen when you conceive, believe and achieve.

I spent a lot of time looking outside myself. I started volunteering from primary school – helping children with disabilities, helping school kids cross the road after 3 pm and doing various jobs for the teachers, such as putting the dishes away. This gave me a sense of purpose when I was lacking it. I still spend a great deal of my spare time volunteering, and I have been the Auckland coordinator for the New Zealand Anti-Vivisection Society (NZAVS), Sea Shepherd New Zealand and No Fixed Abode for several years now. The great thing about volunteering is that it is never too late to start and interestingly, you receive so much from the act of giving.

Martial arts played a huge role in dissipating anger, being disciplined and increasing self-worth. I may not have been able to rely on others for personal safety, but martial arts significantly increased my confidence during times of vulnerability. I've been part of City Kickboxing for a decade now, and they have become my family. There's a wonderful sense of community and connection when you join a martial arts gym.

Meditation also had significant impacts on my mental and emotional well-being when I consistently practiced it. A minimum of 10 minutes per day where I could observe the unstoppable thoughts that came in one after the other, before being able to redirect it to a place of less noise. Our minds can be our biggest enemies with the negative self-talk that tends to dominate the centre stage. I often allocate times to not only meditate but to give myself heartfelt gratitude – change your words, change your world. Be not a victim; be a survivor.

I explored Cognitive Behavioural Therapy (CBT) which helped me analyse my thoughts, feelings, behaviours and physical symptoms. It allowed me to see how they all interacted with another and made me more aware of the various situations. It is important to develop conscious awareness in order to evoke change if change is desired.

In 2017 and 2018, I travelled to Iquitos, Peru, after plenty of research on the plant medicine of Ayahuasca. It is an Amazonian concoction that induces intense introspection and hallucinations. It has been recognised for helping people through depression, anxiety and healing from trauma. I definitely tripped balls and went into the darkest recesses of my mind. Reliving the most excruciating experiences and burning in my own rendition of hell. After nearly two decades of suppression, all my demons came out to play, and I was beside myself. However, something incredible came out of this shit show... for the first time in my life, I held myself and with total conviction said, "I love you, Sylvia". I felt the pain of little Sylvia, and I mourned for her before wholeheartedly embracing her. It was at that moment that I realised that I am my protector and have been all along. That I wasn't responsible for any of the trauma inflicted, but I am responsible for treating myself the way that I deserve; with love and compassion. A truly transformative moment that paved the way for some extraordinary healing. It's not to say the path was straight forward by any means, I was challenged and hit absolute rock bottom before I could work my way back up. But it was all worth it to be free from the chains that had long held me captive. A special mention to David from Maya Ayahuasca and my jungle family who gave me mountains of support.

There was a whole heap of other modalities that I employed on my journey to giving myself more self-care and self-love. Although I like to live with no regrets, one thing I wish I explored earlier was someone to confide in. It was not until I was in my late 20's that I decided to attend therapy consistently, and it has been pivotal in the demise of my depression. To have an unbiased ear that listens and guides without judgement can be super helpful. It is about exploring what works for you and sticking to it. One must also never underestimate the power of intuition – you know, that feeling in your gut that tells you if something feels off? Your body has many weird and wonderful ways of telling you what's up, you have just got to learn to listen to it.

Last but certainly not least – find people that can support you through good times and bad. I spent most of my life alone because I didn't reach out. This is not to say reaching out is on you – we need to live in a world where we ask each other if we are okay rather than expect someone who is hurting to come forward.

However, being proactive when we are in a better place can help substantially when we're not in a good space. Find your tribe. I am now the strongest I have ever been because I have allowed myself to be vulnerable in front of people I love and trust. I don't know where I would be without the love and support from my beautiful soul sisters, family, friends and the LOML from Castlerock.

What does the future hold for me? I try not to look too far ahead, but I have long dreamt of having a sanctuary for animals in need of rescuing. Other than that, continuing with my health and wellness business, cuddling my fur babies and living in the present moment. After all, the now is the only place happiness can be found!

The home is where the heart is. My home is in Aotearoa. My home is in Tāmaki Makaurau. My home is me.

Zac

I was always labelled the naughty child at school as I was always hyper and could never sit still and always had to be the class clown. My mum said she thinks I have ADHD and always have but never been diagnosed with it. I've always turned to drink and drugs as a coping mechanism to block the way I would feel or think. I did this from the age of 15, and first, it was smoking weed and drinking, but as I got older, it turned to cocaine and alcohol.

So, five years ago, I met the woman I cherish and love with all my heart. We got together, and we ended up getting married. She knew I did cocaine but did not realise how bad I could get on it. My first self-harm episode happened when she went out one night, and I was at home alone (just drinking) I drank shit loads that night as I thought she was going to hurt me and play me, as I did this to girls when I was growing up. I thought now I have found someone I am completely in love with; it's going to bite me on the ass like karma getting me back or something. Anyway, she got back, and I accused her of cheating, and one thing led to another, I ended up self-harming and hurt myself quite badly. I ended up going to the hospital, and this time I did not end up with help or anything as I did not want any help. Two years later, my wife and I had a big bust-up because I was on the drugs, and she couldn't handle it, so she said she was divorcing me. This broke my heart; I lost everything....my wife, my home and my self-respect. I spiralled out of control, spending hundreds on drink and drugs. I was staying at my mums' house, and it was an opportunity I felt to cut myself again as she was on holiday, so wouldn't be able to witness. I was broken and so, so low, I didn't want to live anymore, I didn't see any point in living, and I was in the black pit of what felt like no return. Anyway, the police were called, as I contacted my wife, telling her what I did, so she had called the police. Some say its attention-seeking, but to me, I was crying for help from the one who vowed to love me, but she couldn't put herself in a dangerous position by seeing or being with me, due to her having her children and her job.

I see now why she stayed away, but at that point, I was so broken and hurt she didn't want to know me, and I couldn't think of anything else. The person she married and loved she didn't want to be near. So, the police were called after my second self-harm incident, and they took me to the hospital to get stitched up. They then took me to the NHS Oxleas Foundation Trust, where I was referred to Little Brook Hospital in Dartford, which is a psychiatric hospital, as I was registered as living in Kent. I spent one week sectioned and heavily medicated for the week. I felt so monged out from the drugs. I was released into the public under the home treatment team, where I was put on quetiapine and mirtazapine for my low mood disorder and overthinking. It's been nearly two years since I tried to take my life and I can now look back and say to myself what the hell were you doing, but at that moment in time, I did not want to be on this planet anymore.

Two years on, my life has turned around for the better. I've never felt so peaceful and at ease with the world.

My medication is doing what it's supposed to, and I'm happy with life and want to help people going through what I went through. I had a marriage breakdown but also had my own self inner demons beating me up, and now I have got them at bay, where they can no longer get me, and I control my day to day living, not letting my mind take over. I'm one year clean and sober, and I want people to see that you can come out of that bottomless pit and it's not all doom and gloom. Thank you for taking the time to listen to me.

Amy

No Special Story

This is not a special story, it's not unusual or unique, it's not harder or easier than anyone else's, but it's mine. I hope that in sharing my story, others may be inspired to value and perhaps even share theirs.

Written during the Covid-19 lockdown.

Dedicated to my Mum and Dad and Grandma, whom I deeply love and appreciate.

Before I share my story with you, I'd like to take a moment to say thank you to some of the people who have believed in and helped me, many without knowing. For, if it hadn't been for them sharing their kindness and light with me, I wouldn't be here today to tell my story. I vow to pass on the gifts of kindness, compassion and faith in others that have so generously given to me.

Thank you to Jenny at The Lucy Rayner Foundation for giving me the opportunity to give voice to my story. Thank you to Miriam for listening, guiding and empowering me to give voice to my inner child. Thank you to my Art Teachers, Ms Bushby, Mr Jones, Sarah, Will, Dan, Phil, Gill and Jo. Thank you to Rashida and everyone at The Globe Gallery, Katy and Geof at Arcadea Disability Arts and Social changemakers and very special friends Eve and Joe. Thank you to my therapists, Steve, Lindsay and Miriam. Thank you to Amanda and all of the staff at Better Gym, Newcastle, to past bosses, the staff at the local coffee shops, library and community centres. To my number one collaborator, Katie. Thank you to Patrick. To Art School friends, Craig, Laura, Saira and Beverley. Stephanie and Jonathan, Jonathan (Kleverclоggs). Aly, Catherine and everyone at Byker Community Centre. Thank you to David, Ceridwen, Lula, Giri, Sanam, Gini, Sarah, Sunita, Eleni, Robbie, Anete, Zeina, Jessica, Silas, James, Valentina, Amanvir and Laura. Thank you to Jennifer, Isabella and Rula, to Amina at Borderline Books and De Chit Raka at Newcastle Buddhist Centre, to artists Claire, Hannah, Bernard and Matthew and to dear friends Ghana and Allan. Thank you to my Dad and Grandma, who always believed in me. To my step-Mum, Jackie, my aunties Nick and Jo, and uncles Davey, Ollie and Tony and Martin and Julie-Ann. Thank you to my Mum for creating my little sister who is my one and only Super Star and thank you to her family, Amiee, Tom and lovely little Hazel. A special thanks to Rachael who has been there for me throughout. I hope that we will continue to share and support each other on our journeys of healing and growth long into the future.

To all of my mentors, Thank you.

Born in Ashington in 1992 and brought up in Blyth, Northumberland. As I remember, I had a financially poor but happy, loving and creative childhood up until the age of 10. My Dad was studying his Fine Arts degree, and so I was always surrounded by paintings and would play around the big sculptures in the garden, notably a huge colourful wooden wigwam. My Mum worked a few part-time chef jobs, she loved cooking, and we used to do a lot of craft activities together. We used to visit my Grandma once or twice a year down south, and this was always a magical and loving experience. I was shy, but very chatty when comfortable, according to my early school reports. As an only child, I spent a lot of time playing alone immersed in imagination. I was 10 when my Mum and Dad split up. I went to live with my Mum and her boyfriend, who was a family friend. Let's call him Dave. Dave made his living selling tat like tinny headphones, plug heads and other miscellaneous crap trapped in the steamed-up atmosphere of weathered, well-travelled plastic packaging, at boot sales from his rusty and probably uninsured white van. Where he acquired his merchandise was a mystery, and I didn't care, especially when free toys were concerned. The house was suffused with mountains of cardboard boxes crammed with second hand Happy Meal toys, damp tamagotchis and chipped tea sets. Plant pots, cigarette lighters and cutlery bound in Sellotape. You know the guy I mean; tall, thin with a spiky greying beard. He could be very funny and charming, and he used to go on adventures to India and South Africa, bringing back beautiful rugs and ornaments which my Mum loved! The purpose of his excursions, however, was to smuggle heroin. I heard he was quite well known for bringing heroin into Blyth in the early '90s when we developed a significant opiate problem. My Mum had long curly hair down to her legs; she coloured it in rainbows of reds and purples that framed her fresh freckled face, adorned with big round glasses. She was beautiful. She wore velvet gowns of all different colours and had the most contagious and whooping laugh. She was so nurturing and understanding of people, always there to offer counsel, never judgemental. She aspired to work in social care, helping people process their trauma through art activities. She loved to cook, and before she left work through mental and physical illness she worked part-time as a chef, this experience was visibly stressful, and she struggled to cope with the social dramas and pressure. I believe my Mum was attracted to heroin to help with the debilitating arthritis in her back as well as her anxiety. She was 30 at the time and was later in life diagnosed with Bipolar Disorder.

With a wad of money stolen from an Indian fabric covered cylinder, I would go food shopping at our local convenience store, equipped with an always-packed rucksack containing spare clothes, a bus timetable and a Happy Meal Lion King Simba, named Johnny, who joined me everywhere. I would have fearlessly run away if it were not necessary to protect my Mum. Filling a trolly with cereal, bread, margarine, chocolate, apples, chicken slices and jam I felt like an undercover agent, no one asked why a child had so much cash, nor as I recall, did they care. The final stage of the mission was to sneak the bags of food into the house undetected, and if I was caught, Dave would know I had been stealing, and the bomb would once again be ignited. Eating large amounts of food alone provided me with a feeling of independence and comfort, I would sit my teddies in a circle and have a picnic, they loved it! I also had a toaster in my bedroom in which I'd cook potato waffles and toast, and this kid wasn't messing about. I would put a chest of draws up against my bedroom door to keep out intruders; this was particularly useful when I no longer had a door. The bathroom also didn't have a door, and so I had to use a bucket in my room and empty it when the night was still. I used to eat until my tummy felt to pop, stuffing white bread smothered in cheap margarine into my mouth drowning out the sound of my Mum's screaming and crying, the smashing of glass and the thundering roar of Dave hurling abuse. More often than not I would leave my bedroom to find the whole house had been smashed up; kitchen utilities like the washing machine lying dead on its side in the hallway, the whole contents of the cupboards sprawled across the floor. All the plates and cups were smashed, the always-closed curtains hung diagonally as the rail had been ripped from the wall, we had to nail them up after that. There were no longer any doors inside. I slept in my school uniform and wouldn't use the bath without a door.

There was a phone box at the top of the street where I would sometimes call the police, secretly you understand, as this act of disobedience came with particularly grim consequences. I remember returning from the phone box, having backed out of my gallant but essentially foolish endeavour, and there stood another 10-year-old girl, surrounded by other kids from the estate. They wanted to batter me, "Fucking hippie!" "You're soft as shit!" "Look at ah hair man, what an absolute skank," and before I had time to devise a reaction, I was dragged to the tarmac by my ponytail. Scorching hot panic pumped through my veins, "Fight, Fight, Fight!" They chanted, "Get off me!" I yell, hoping a responsible adult would hear, "Stamp on her head!" I screamed as loud as I could, like a baby bird, fallen from an equally perilous nest. To my disappointment, no one came. My Mum's advice was always to run away; I squirmed my way out from under the snarling insults, fists clenching clumps of my hair and trampling Rockports and ran. The drum pounded harder and louder as I approached number 30. What will be happening inside my house? I ran past my door, past the sandpit park, past the local shop and onto a field where I stopped, I wasn't allowed out further than the street. I lay on the grass and gazed into the sky, I wished I had my rucksack with me, I would leave right now and get on a bus, and then a train. I imagined myself on the train, I knew how to buy a ticket, and I had money in my bag. I imagined calling my Grandma from a payphone, and I knew her number. It made me happy to imagine how proud she would be of me travelling all of that way by myself, she would hug me and cut me a slice of Victoria Sponge, and she would sit and listen as I told her all about what had been happening and then we would come and save my Mum and live down south and... I had to go back. I wasn't allowed to tell Grandma anything, and I couldn't leave my Mum. I sat in my bedroom, no longer disillusioned by my glittery and hopeful daydreams. As the roars became more intense, so did the intensity of my distractions; pulling my hair out, hitting my head against the wall, having what I now understand to be panic attacks. Jonny, a physical manifestation of my imaginary friend, would always provide reassurance that everything was going to be ok and that I was not alone. Dave was physically violent to both my Mum and me in different ways, about which I am not going to go into detail. When I was 13, I went to the police about how he had violated me, but as the story too often goes, there wasn't enough evidence to prosecute.

After around one year, we fled down south to stay in a women's refuge where my Mum had a nervous breakdown. Caused, I imagine by the combination of fleeing an abusive relationship she was attached to, addiction and withdrawal, fear and probably post-traumatic stress. I moved between staying with my Dad and Grandma, and by 13 resided with my Dad in Blyth for high school. A great terror was ignited inside of me when facing the prospect of seeing my

Mum; I had refused any contact with her since our separation. It was when the social workers encouraged to contact that I first seriously considered suicide. My life of secrecy and stealing continued through my teenage hood. I carried a knife at one point as I fled the now bigger and more organised group of bullies, orchestrated by the same now teenagers who lived in my and my Mum's old street, reliving the fear of attack in a different environment. I began drinking, smoking and skiving school. It was fun, and amongst this chaos, I had friends, boyfriends, and tried drugs where I experienced the most liberating of euphoria. On a weekend we danced, sang, laughed, and fantasised about the futures most of us knew were out of grasp. Though deep down somewhere, I knew I could transcend this life, and I knew it would be through art. We camped and played, fell in and out of love, built dens in the woods while skiving school, free in nature to be ourselves. I understood that the bullies were just like me, traumatised with no idea how to cope. I didn't like fighting, and I didn't know how to fight. I tried negotiating with them, that just pissed them off even more. I started cutting myself daily, I hated myself, I developed Bulimia at 14, but didn't know what that was; this eating disorder grew to consume my life. I have always known that my Dad loves and idolises me unconditionally, but my secrecy and emotional detachment meant he couldn't connect with or properly support me because he didn't know what was happening. At 14 I reconnected with my Mum and saw her once or twice a year. Homelessness and heroin had ravaged her life. Our separation had ripped her apart, and she was clearly traumatised by both our separation and her relationship with Dave. Nevertheless, we began to nurture a new relationship, and for that, I am very grateful.

In my middle and numerous high schools, the Art Room was my refuge, I was a hard worker, and so the art teachers usually took a liking to me. I skived almost every day throughout high school, and I would sneak into the school for my art lessons, my art teacher would see me coming and open the back entrance and act as if nothing had happened, what an absolute legend! With a compassionate tilt of the head he would ask if I needed to talk, an offer I'd always politely reject before hopping back over the school fence, I skived so often that the schools stopped trying. This was the birth of my relationship with art and I made a vow to myself to pursue it, I stuck in for the final three months of high school, attended all of the revision classes and studied like I had never before to get the grades that would allow me to study art at college. Much to my and my teacher's astoundment, I only got one of my 11 GCSE's below a C, Food Tech, if you're wondering! The realisation that hard work can have consequences such as these was empowering. I pursued art at college and was diagnosed with dyslexia. I received 1:1 writing tuition and consistently got top marks, I worked, and worked, and worked, all day, all night. My Bulimia by this point had become a three-time a day habit that I had no intention of kicking. I created bodies of work about addiction, psychological entrapment and followed a descent into fiction and immersia, where the magic lived. 'The Artist's Mother' was the last piece of work I made at Newcastle College, and it represented two years of creative recovery. Although unspoken, I know that my art teachers understood the therapeutic value of art and despite the role of the therapist not being what they had signed up for, I was always supported and guided with an unwavering attention and, for that I will always be grateful. I didn't believe in myself but they did, and through die-hard determination, I got a place to study BA Fine Art at Chelsea College of Arts in London, which was and is still quite unbelievable. Despite my illusion of fierce independence, the transition away from this tight community felt like that of being cut from the umbilical cord. I eventually settled into the new Art School, and the experience became radically mind-opening and life-changing, as well as a relentless duel between hard work, lack of education, low self-esteem and Bulimia, though, I think I hid that well. The fire that I had discovered within, that I shielded with all my might, in addition to the top-class tutoring carried me through the difficulties. I knew, above all else, that I was an artist. Very proactive and completely dedicated, I could see a brighter future opening up before me, and I felt truly fantastic.

In my final year, the eating disorder led me to being kicked out of my accommodation, and because I was spending much of my money on visiting my Mum, who was suicidal, after having her second child taken away soon after birth, I became homeless. My Mum's situation evolved an ineluctable presence in both my consciousness and routine. An unwavering tension pulled at the taut thread that distinguished the boundaries between my past and present; like a beaten guitar string, it was one vibrational ping away from snapping. I sat by a drained, vaulted pool. An Edwardian arched ceiling framed it in the derelict Haggerston Baths. Tags and graffiti adorned the walls and innards of the pool, in the daytime illuminated by a corridor of the skylight. I grappled with piles of scrawled notes, photocopies of pages of books - notes upon sketches upon notes: A note next to a highlighted sentence read: 'Maurice Merleau- Ponty suggests that phenomenological experience is defined by the interactions between the phenomena and context in that specific place and time, and not by any single attribute alone. Merleau-Ponty in The Phenomenology of Perception, 1999 writes: "When through the water's thickness I see the tiling at the bottom of a pool, I do not see it despite the water and the reflections there; I see it through them and because of them."' My gaze drifted across the lapsed pool, A sign read, "SHALLOW END", the thirsty space a geo-psychological map of my psyche, as perceived through my bleak and dejected phthalo lenses. 'Am I not clever enough? Educated? Is it my dyslexia that's causing this academic chaos, this lack of meaning? A lack of self-discipline?' I explored the premises, distracting from the self- deprecating churnings of my mind. Secrets seemed to be suspended in the blackened shadows blanketing corridors of redundant showers; portentous and aesthetically stomach-churning, in a good way. Rooms upon rooms, high-reaching walls shedding generations of durable paint. A mattress and a book, a mattress and an ashtray sprinkled with tiny silver bottles, a crumpled-up sleeping bag cowering in the corner, burnt-out candles, a coca-cola bong, a used needle. An interminable labyrinth littered with abandoned activity. Situated two basements down was an engine room housing three original coal-fired, 28ft Lancashire boilers, said to have been reclaimed from a ship. It was like being inside of a 19th-century spaceship. Haggerston baths were closed after suffering bomb attacks during WW2. There have been recent petitions for the regeneration of the leisure facilities, situated in the poorest part of Hackney Borough, but, as the story so often goes, it was not a funding priority. One floor up, in the first basement two enraged men with a vicious black dog, baring razor sharp teeth were arguing in a different language, about drugs I was later informed. 'There are no bad dogs, just bad owners', I wondered, what brought these men to this moment in their lives?

I found a quiet space to call my Mum. I didn't tell her about what had been happening, she asked about my schoolwork and said she was so proud of me, that I was so intelligent and talented. She always was 'over the top'. I said, "I don't feel clever; I feel undereducated." She told me how far I had come, how hard working I am and how impressed everyone is going to be when I have a big exhibition, "imagine it, all of your big paintings on the walls and everyone has come to see them because they love you and they love your work, and if they don't like you or your work then they can bog off, it doesn't matter." I laughed as silent tears filled my eyes. "It will be a big whooping party all about my superstar artist munchkin!" It always put her on a high when talking about my art and studies at Chelsea. It was only the day before that I had been talking her out of suicide. I would send her photographs of my work and printouts of my essays and evaluations which she had pinned up all over the flat alongside photographs of us together and of me as a baby. "You are so talented my darling, so you just keep working hard and the people who matter will see it." "How are you, Mum?" "Up and down, I'm waiting for therapy, and my doctor said it would be months and months." "I'll come and see you soon, and we can go on a walk with a picnic?" "Yes, darling, I can't wait." I sat in silence for a while. The black dog seemed to take refuge in my mind. I later shot a film following the dog through the concrete maze, pursuing the idea of the unkempt and abandoned labyrinth being a geo-psychological metaphor for my state of mind.

I found freedom in having no fixed abode, no rent to worry about, and only the abundant bag on my back to sustain me. I sensed its bond with the always packed rucksack of my childhood; I had finally been given the opportunity to run away. I explored London on foot through day and night with an aimless licence, and it did not cost anything to use my eyes. I sat on curbs with homeless women drinking coffee, and as we exchanged snippets of stories. I painted some of them in the sanctuary of my studio, immersed and free. I steered clear of alcohol and drugs while homeless for all but one night where I attended a party in New Cross Gate. Drenched in disillusionment and gassy Whitestripe lager I danced amongst the crowd of my euphoric cohort, and I spun as the disco lights washed my bagless body. 1, 2, 3 am, the crowd thinned, I had to collect my bag from the reception of a hotel in Marble Arch, that's a story for another day. A man who had been at the bus stop got on the bus. I arrived at Marble Arch after three-night busses and collected my bag. The man from the bus stop had been following me. I told the security and went to the toilets in the naive hope he would be gone when I came out. He wasn't, and my heart went boom when I saw him standing there. I reassure myself that the security will stop us. We walked out into the dead night. I walked with intention, and he followed, 'keep walking until sunrise' my nebulous mind proposed. My phone was dead. I shout at him on Oxford Street; "I know you're following me; I'll call the police if you don't leave me alone!", creating a spectacle to alert the piddling crowd of bystanders. I don't remember arriving on Oxford St or at Kings Cross or getting into a taxi or arriving at his house. "I'm not sleeping with you," I asserted. He slept on the sofa, and I collapsed clothed onto the bed, foolishly deciding to sleep a couple of hours before leaving. I awoke with my phone on charge in my hand. It was 8 am, and he was inside of me. I froze. After a few minutes of familiar defilement, my body vaulted up in disgust. I heaved my belongings into the bathroom and locked the door. I showered, brushed my teeth thoroughly, applied makeup and got dressed emerging packed for an immediate exit. "I can make you breakfast before you go?" He said, as if nothing out of the ordinary had happened, "That was rape", I replied. The sun beamed down into my sunken hungover eyes as I walked through an unknown estate, eventually emerging at Arsenal tube station. Had I been spiked? I could not recollect. I told a friend who told my tutor, and within days I was rehoused in student accommodation with a grant to cover the rent. "You need to go to the police," my friend insisted, "there's no point" I repeated. At the police station I gave a detailed statement, directing them to CCTV cameras, security guards and busses travelled with a vague timeline and a sketch of the man with a good likeness. This was too much for my mind to process, what with my studies, not having a home and my Mum's mental health. I called my Mum. I didn't want to, and I feared not knowing what state of mind she was going to be in, would she be drunk, ecstatic, suicidal? She was the latter; she cried and cried, mourning her lost child. "She will be safe and happy, I just know it, and you still have me, and I love you so much." "I know darling, and I love you so so so much, but I don't know how I can live like this anymore..." We talked for over an hour. A couple of weeks later I was informed by the police that there was not enough evidence and they couldn't find the man. The dissertation deadline was fast approaching, and the pressure of completing what I had spent eight years working to achieve sunk me into a dream-like haze. I visited the college counsellor. "I feel like I want to kill myself," I told her, "the only reason I haven't thrown myself off a bridge is that I need to finish my degree." I hadn't told anyone this and saying it out loud made it feel more real. I told her I was worried that my Mum was going to take her life, she said I was exaggerating the situation in my mind. I felt angry and resentful, I felt like I was in the wrong place, that people here don't understand people like me, from my background, and I had to make significant effort to not allow that working-class chip on my shoulder to deepen. I had to get this degree, and I had to prove to myself that I was just as deserving to be here like everyone else and I wasn't going to be defined by where I grew up or how my life had earlier unfolded. I decided to stop contacting my Mum to focus upon its completion. I had recently topped her phone up so, if she calls, I thought, I will answer. Two weeks later and two weeks before the dissertation deadline, I was informed that my Mum had taken her life. The counsellor later apologised for her mistake for which I was grateful and held no hard feelings, for we are all learning.

I entered Tate Britain in the knowledge that I was going to see JMW Turner's paintings. I was not in the mood to look at a painting. I was looking for something, anything. As I stood feeling quietly green-eyed, I was slowly seduced by thumbnail spaces of mark-making. I became conscious of time passing. Had it been ten minutes, had I been at this one long enough? An unnecessary self-consciousness. Subtle and beautiful. It wasn't trying to be beautiful or to impress me or keep my attention or move me on. It just was; more than a wall object or an energetic landscape painting with flags pointing toward realism and social and industrial documentation. An undistinguishable feeling of longing came over me as I allowed the painting to wash and soothe my trembling stupor. The way he works with distance is sublime; almost visible figuration wrapped in an air that permeates the space between myself and the horizon. Clear visibility opens and closes at the pace of what I imagine inhalation and exhalation to be during deep sleep; slow deep bodily time. Inhale, exhale. Open, close. Forth and back. "Here. Is Turner here? Something other than a painting is here," my intuition murmured. The plane was dashed and dotted with marks of acknowledgment of his surroundings, but also, acknowledgement of himself and his medium. Here and then gone, following the momentum of a dragging tide, it hummed. I felt reassured.

When my Mum died, I was in shock, and my bulimic behaviour began to exceed itself in both frequency and veracity. I felt guilty that I had stopped contacting her, responsible. I felt angry that her situation had once again steamrolled over my life. I didn't want to be a self-absorbed victim, I wanted to be a fighter, a survivor... an artist. But I felt like a victim, just like my Mum. She wouldn't have wanted this, but this wasn't about me. I drew a great deal of personified spoons, and I drew portraits of my Mum, some quite harrowing, others somewhat angelic and I drew the bathroom where she was found. I submitted my dissertation returned to Blyth on a gap year; it felt like a return to ground zero. I would cycle through my and my Mum's old street. She still talked about that time, trapped in a loop of psychological trauma. 'He did this to her', I thought, the psychopathic bastard, and he did this to me, and I have carried the increasingly heavy weight of my Mum's pain ever since. I received CBT support for my eating disorder for the first time and would bring food diaries and drawings to my appointments. I was having frequent panic attacks, sometimes taking up my therapist's offer to call him during. He would ask me to slow my breathing, notice my environment, “What can you see?” “A tree”, “Focus on the tree, what colour is it? What does the bark feel like to touch?” This never helped in the way I wanted it to. It took me back to the present moment, reminded me that I was on a long path of healing. I didn’t understand the significance of this at the time. I desired healing at my core, my inner child needed to be heard, understood and loved. I didn’t know that either.

In an old office block reclaimed by social charities, I was invited to be an artist in residence by the founders of the building project, who organised this community space with the intention of saving lives. Collaborating with the residents, I led interviews and art workshops where we explored the value of this new community. The three-month project culminated in an exhibition entitled ‘Birds of Different Feather’, and one week later I moved back to London to rejoin Chelsea.

I rejoined a different year group and was confronted by how much both I and my coursework had changed: everything felt foreign and distant. I could grasp no connection with Guy Debord’s reflections on The Spectacle, Fredrick Jameson’s analysis of Post-Modernity and capitalism, Walter Benjamin’s deconstruction of art, reproduction and politics; I could perceive only one omnipresent aura. Mum, Mum, Mum.

There was the work I felt like I ought to create to be in with any chance of getting my predicted grades, and the work I felt I had to make, the only work I could make, I explained in a tutorial: “I cannot articulate a connection between my past research and coursework and this new work.” “Can you tell me about the new work?” my theory tutor of three years responded inquisitively, “It’s about my Mum.”

It was an abstract body of large paintings that fell silent in group critiques. They followed pre-studies about someone being unable to swim in a murky pool surrounded by burnt spoons. Two large green planes represented the water, and another painting on MDF was nailed over the front to give the impression of an inaccessible space. I graduated in 2016.

When I graduated, I had achieved what I had aspired to do. I was working as an artist and setting up projects, working with some fine collaborators in art galleries and community spaces, but despite this, I slowly felt the meaning drain from my life, what was going to stop me from taking my life now? I had been running from my grief, and a few rejected project funding applications down the line, I reached total burnout. I had identified with art as an identity: when the work was 'bad' I was bad, when it was rejected, as was I and when I wasn't creating, well, I was of no value. When the mask of the artist was taken away, I was still the child who snuck around to survive hiding the ED and depression, revealing that I did not understand how to care for myself inside or out in a healthy or maintainable way. During the long depression following my Mum's death, I fell into unexpected but prompted situations, like I was trying to relive my Mum's experiences, to understand what led to her death and to be close to her. The way she had to sell her body for narcotics, her homelessness and her depression. At the peak of this depression, I was smoking weed every day, and taking other drugs while becoming immersed in progressively more unsafe situations. I needed to feel something, anything to fill the vacuous black hole in my chest.

I remember it was a winter morning. I awoke with lungs like frostbitten flesh and lit a spliff. On the inhalation, I pulled the cloud of smoke into my body, on exhalation, I let go of the load and became momentarily immersed in a tide of relief. Most days I would drink coffee and fall out of the front door in a swirling haze of caffeination and THC. It didn't become a problem until I began to find my sober life intolerable, so I did it every day for a while; that's why they call it a habit. I don't think it becomes an addiction until you try to stop and can't. Walking into town, I was confronted by a deep and familiar emptiness. It was an insecure feeling, of needing to cry or shout but not knowing how, the feeling of lack and loss, perhaps of my Mum or, of control. I looked around at the people going about their lives, were they too hollow? If their exterior appearance were peeled away, would the shadow of their hungry ghost be exposed? Depression is a different spectrum altogether, of reality, where everything is in a state of suffering and lack - where everything but the truth that the depression reveals, is fake. I missed my Mum, the thought stirred up my insides, how I longed to cry like a baby in her arms. She left a long time before her untimely death, and if she were here now, I thought, there would be nothing she could do to help me and still, nothing I could do to help her. I mourned myself, the person I was no longer becoming. Later that night, I once again found myself having consumed a stupendous quantity of food rammed down with the desire of oblivion and intention of purging. A clump of undigested food formed a pack in my chest before pushing its way up my throat and landing in the toilet followed by a gush of liquid. I was reminded that this is what I am now. There was no escape from this eating disorder from this depression.

Some weeks later, I was greeted by an unfamiliar suicidal feeling: This, coupled with the helplessness and self-disgust, gave me clarity. Alone in my flat, I sat on the floor with a large sheet of paper where I wrote notes to those I love. I took a massive overdose, only to have an eventual sinking sensation in my body 8 hours later, devastated as gravity pulled me back down to my living room floor. I felt a slow drawback to consciousness; the effects of the overdose were wearing off. In my slurred delirium I called for an ambulance, as soon as I got off the phone, I vomited an unimaginably vile and toxic bile. Two paramedics arrived; they helped me to the ambulance. I lay down in the ambulance, and a man talked to me about what had happened. I was sitting in a wheelchair in a corridor drifting in and out of sleep for what felt like hours, and someone kindly brought a biscuit. Two nurses took me into a room, "So what was this", I vaguely remember her asking me, "were you getting high?" I didn't like her attitude and got upset. I asked her to be understanding and not judgemental, "this was real", I said, among other things that I don't remember. She apologised profusely. I was discharged at 3 or 4 am with no money for a taxi and still not of a sound state of mind. I stumbled through the night following my instincts on how to get home, I knew it wasn't very far, I just had to find a place I recognised, and then I'd be fine. That walk put a lot of things into perspective. 'I am 26' I thought, 'an adult responsible for myself... is this the life I'm going to live...Am I going to live?' As I stumbled across the gusty, blackened Town Moor, I travelled back in time, back to mine and my Mum's street, back to college, to Chelsea, to Haggerston Baths, I remembered the dreams I once had, the passion for art, for helping people. How was I going to get out of this psychological mess? Following this, I was fortunate enough to receive support from the Community Mental Health team and soon after I also started a course of Psycho-dynamic therapy, to which I entered with a drastically altered attitude. I knew where I would end up if I didn't pursue a better life, and I knew the pain that this would cause those whom I love.

For the final sections of this story I have been asked to respond to two questions: 'What do I wish for my future?' and 'What advice do I offer to the reader?' These ideas have been the most difficult to articulate because like everyone else, I am still on my journey of healing and growth, but I'll embrace the uncertainty and give it my best shot.

So, the three most significant lessons that have been bestowed upon me are the values of a supportive community, mental and physical self-care and the transformative role of art and creativity and this has led me a new aspiration to set up some form of alternative community art school where creativity and well-being can be explored and practiced.

I will always be an artist; it is my way of understanding and processing the world. For me, art offers opportunities to make connections; between ideas, people and experiences and although it can often be created in isolation it is important for the work to be shared, experienced and responded to. I hope to get a studio amongst a community of artists keeping my feelers out for exciting collaborations. Art exhibitions, artist talks, creative workshops and tutorials with visiting artists at university have played significant roles in my journey as an artist, and I aspire to share ideas to create spaces that encourage creativity and personal growth, just like those aforementioned. I have applied to study an MA in Art Psychotherapy, where I hope to have the opportunity to bring together my experiences to help others. It was working with adults with varying disabilities and mental health struggles where I was reminded of the transformative role that creativity, art and community can play in supporting and developing people's communication skills, confidence and healing. I hope to be able to develop my skills as an arts creative workshop facilitator and to work in a host of different environments; from visualisation and mental well-being in the workplace to rehabilitation and confidence-building in prisons and hostels, working to develop an art and therapeutic practice with a focus upon well-being, the prevention of suicide, the healing of grief and trauma and creative empowerment while raising a wider awareness and understanding of such experiences. I have also just started my driving lessons and hope that one day in the future I could get a car or a van to travel in for work. Yoga and physical exercise are helping me to build a healthy relationship between my body and mind, giving me the opportunity to develop new habits while recovering from the eating disorder. Sometimes I feel like a child learning how to live a good life, it can be repetitive and frustrating, but the results of these efforts can be indescribably empowering, even when the result is getting back up after a fall. Where once I was too overcome by the fear of failure, now I have gathered enough evidence to know that I have the power within me to learn and change the direction of my life. So, I will protect my flame from being extinguished with all of my valor and allow it to guide me to and through whatever this unpredictable life has in store.

WHAT ADVICE CAN I GIVE TO THE READER?

Advice is a tricky thing, what helps me isn't necessarily going to be the thing that helps you, or it might be, but not right now. But once again, embracing the uncertainty of my answers, I will share with you some things that I have found helpful. When I was first introduced to mindfulness, I thought what a load of old tosh, I don't want to live in the moment, it's awful, that's the point. However, in the years to come I started to discover that all of those negative beliefs I had about myself and my situation, the ideas that held me back, that told me, 'I'm a crap artist', 'too fat to take my jacket off', to go on holiday or to visit a gym.' 'Too jittery to be tolerated, too loud, too shy; not photogenic, clever, charming or funny enough, not enough.' Those thoughts are not really who I am, deep down, and I do not need to heed their destructive advice or allow them to define who I am.

This was a painstaking and slow process of realisation and that microscopic iota of hope that there could be a way out of that reality, was my guiding glowing grain. Mindfulness, slowing to observe the moment as it is now, whether that be through simple breathing exercises, meditation, yoga or a nice little walk was my way of staying connected with the idea that there still was, but an infinitesimal speck of hope. Through the ups and downs of life, the fleck became more perceptible, and as it matured so did the nihilistic commentator in my head; "that glossy little dot your following is just a figment of your imagination." Imagination, I pondered. It has been through imagining a better future that has, in part, allowed me to participate in a life now headed on a more positive and empowered path. The imagination, my friends, is not to be underestimated, and it is not out of your control. That little nebula of imaginary hope has led to real, measurable results, and if you haven't found your spec of optimism yet, or are struggling to keep it in sight, please postpone the downward spiral of despair, and trust that it exists for you. You always have been and always will be enough. Mindfulness can be a powerful tool, and perhaps you may try it out sometime.

A significant change opened up in my life when, through a course of Psycho-dynamic therapy, I began to give voice and understanding to the past versions of myself, starting with 'the inner child'. I would travel back in time in my mind and listen to how my 10-year-old self was feeling, why she started to eat and self-harm. She didn't understand what was happening, but I do. My therapist would ask; 'Do you hate that little girl; do you think that she was bad or ugly or stupid?' 'No...' So, my second piece of advice would be to find a way to give the past versions of yourself a voice, and this does not only go for your childhood. 10, 20 or 50 years old, your past selves deserve a voice, understanding and love, and through my experience, they won't settle until they get it. This could be explored through therapy, or through writing it down and sharing it with someone you trust. You could even call the Samaritans, and they are always there to listen to a friend in need. 116123

My next piece of wisdom is to try things out. Not all counsel given to you is going to be appropriate, but sometimes there is no harm in trying, remember to use your intuition and common sense when considering others' advice. Seek good advice. Speaking candidly with my GP and a fitness instructor at my local Better gym turned out to be two of the most radically shifting conversations in challenging my eating disorder. Two books that have really helped me are The Artist's Way by Julia Cameron and A New Earth by Eckart Tolle.

Practice gratitude - this doesn't mean feeling guilty that you have more than someone else or resentful that someone has more than you. It's just acknowledging what you do have and giving it some appreciation.

Seek out a community that supports your personal growth and healing.

Find a creative outlet, whether it's cooking, gardening, painting or keeping a journal; find an activity that offers you the opportunity to become immersed in doing. Perhaps you can learn and develop a skill and explore your imagination, who knows what jewels and treasures you might find in there. And remember, take everything one baby step at a time, find focus and be kind to yourself, you have already come so far.

Now that this is written and ready to be sent out into the world, my next challenge is going to be to share my story with some of those very close to me who don't know much of what has been written, so, yeah, wish me luck on that.

Caroline

My name is Caroline, and I live in Headcorn, Kent with my husband Mark, my brother Jack, and our three cats Millie, Bliss and Amber. Last month I turned 60, and so my mental health journey has been a long one with all the messy ups and downs of life. The way my awareness of my own mental health has evolved, is similar to peeling back the layers of an onion, each layer taking me deeper and closer to the truth, as well as revealing another piece of the jigsaw and shedding light on earlier stages of my journey.

My perception of myself and my mental health journey has changed radically over the years; I will try and make sense of it for you.

I was the first of four children; my mother was only 21years old when I was born. My father always wanted a son, and he had three girls before he got the son he longed for. By the time my Mum was 26 years old, she had three young children and a baby to look after.

It would be easy to describe our childhood as idyllic, with parents who loved us, a cat, a rabbit, and two guinea pigs and a large garden to play in including our very own fairy ring of mushrooms, a swing and a sandpit. However, there were also a few events that happened when I was aged about 6 or 7 that had very unfortunate consequences for both my mental health as well as creating an urgent need to look after my younger siblings.

My father was a busy GP who worked hard to provide us with a public-school education so that we would have the best opportunities in life and my mother, as well as answering the phone for my father (yes doctors got calls from patients at home in those days), she also had her hands full looking after all of us. She was a great mother in helping us to develop hobbies, such as ice skating, riding, golf, swimming, tennis, painting and sewing. She told me many years later that she had wanted to find something that each one of us was good at.

About five years ago, out of the blue, my Mum recalled a memory of a family trip to Stourhead (a National Trust house and gardens) in the mid-60s. I had complained that I had indigestion from a very green and unripe apple I had picked up in the gardens and eaten. As my Mum correctly remembered, I had complained for days afterwards that the apple had given me "indigestion forever". I was only 6 or 7 at the time.

Five years ago, aged 55, I knew the real reason for my 6-year old's stomach-ache; I had been suffering from extreme anxiety. However, I had no wish to say anything about it to my mother as I didn't want to rehash an old story. She didn't appear to know why she had suddenly remembered it, and I didn't want her to think that I was blaming her or my father.

Our minds, bodies and emotions are all connected. It was to be another 26 years before that little girl of 6 understood enough to start her healing journey and begin to learn how to calm the anxiety in her stomach.

As well as the other events, at about the same time, I also overheard my father talking about his plans for me going to Oxford University. This was a tremendous pressure to put on such a young child, although I'm not sure he even knew that I overheard him talking about it when I was so young.

My father came from a medical dynasty, and in 2001 the Journal of the Royal College of Physicians of Edinburgh published an article called "The Russells of Edinburgh: A Medical Dynasty". My grandfather William Ritchie Russell was the first Professor of Neurology and founder of the School of Neurology at Oxford University. His father before him, William Russell, had been both Professor of Clinical Medicine at Edinburgh University and President of the Royal College of Physicians of Edinburgh. Relatives, family friends and school teachers would often tell me how clever I was and ask if I was going to follow in Dad's footsteps and become a doctor.

It wasn't until much later in life that I realised that not only was my Dad projecting his unfulfilled hopes and aspirations onto me, but that he would also have felt a lot of pressure from his own family to become a successful doctor himself.

When I was seven my mother's father, (called Grandpa to distinguish him from Grandad, who was my father's father), paid the fees for us all to move to a prep school. I was generally happy there, but a couple of incidents stood out for me.

One summer, when we were rehearsing in the sunken garden, I got sunstroke, and I spent the afternoon in the school sanatorium. During the afternoon I was sick in the sink, and because I was anxious about the adults not believing me, I put the plug in to save the evidence. But then after a while, I realised that it would look strange and that I was being silly. This anxiety was even worse than not being believed, and so I pulled the plug out. Today, 52 years later, I can still feel the sliminess of the sick, and the pieces of food in the sick, as I put my hand in to pull out the plug.

I continued to fear that people wouldn't believe me for most of my childhood and teenage years. If anyone accused me of anything, I would blush even if it had nothing to do with me.

It was around the same time period that I had started to realise that my parents generally didn't support us in the way I would have liked. If I ever had any difficulty with my schoolwork and asked for help, I was told that I had to do it on my own because otherwise, I would be cheating.

When I was nine, Grandpa died. I don't remember much about how my parents broke the news, but I do remember there were lots of hushed conversations over the next few days. It wasn't until many years later that I learnt that he had ended his own life. To this day, I know nothing about how he did it. I asked my mother about his death recently; it was a very brief conversation in which I learnt that he had had problems with his heart and was upset about no longer being able to be out on the golf course with his friends. Suicide was a taboo subject while I was growing up.

When I was 11, I went away to a girls' boarding school, and I can still remember laying at night, in the narrow metal-framed bed, worrying about what might happen to my sisters and brother if I wasn't there to look after them.

I also worried about doing well enough to get to Oxford. As a result, I worked hard in all subjects, but particularly sciences. Every summer we had exams, and if you got more than 60% in all subjects, then you were given a special certificate. I got one every year.

After my O-levels I changed school. The girls' school was not good at teaching sciences, and I wanted to move, so my Dad suggested I went to the boys' school where he was the school doctor. Going to a boys' school wasn't ideal as I was only 15½ at the time and painfullly shy, but I agreed in order to get the science teachers who would give me a better chance of getting to Oxford.

Other things were upsetting me. In my A-level term, a couple of the girls sent me to Coventry. One time a group of them, girls and boys, were chatting in the study next door. I overheard someone saying, "oh she's not in there is she"; someone came and pushed open the door and then ran away laughing. Other times, if I turned around when I was walking up the stairs to our study, I would find the boys making faces at me behind my back.

This was an excruciating time of my life, I would have internal debates with myself about what was wrong with me, and then I would be upset, because I thought they were being mean. And then I started to play right/wrong games in my mind. Who was right, and who was wrong? It wasn't an easy time, and later I would realise that it had left me with a subconscious belief that there was something wrong with me.

Despite all of that, at the time, I counted myself lucky (did I mention that my mother always looked for the silver lining?). There was a boy in the year below me who was suffering far more than me.

He was being bullied, and sometimes it got physical. He mixed a bit with my group of friends outside school. He was always pleasant and kind to me when I met him, and I felt sorry for him that he was having such a hard time at school.

When it came to studying for my A- levels, I was a complete workaholic and worried all the time that I wouldn't be good enough to get into Oxford. As part of our exam preparation, all our teachers sent off for the preceding three years of past exams, so that we could get an idea of what to expect. I was so anxious about getting to Oxford, that this wasn't enough for me, I actually sent away to the examination board for the exam papers for a further three years, so I could look for patterns over the whole six previous years' exams. This will give you an idea of how desperate I was to get to Oxford and please my Dad.

It was a huge relief when the A-level results came out; I got 3 grade A's in Maths, Physics and Chemistry and a grade 2 in Chemistry S-level. But now I started to worry even more about the Oxford Entrance exams.

Over the summer, I had also realised that I had no idea what I wanted to do for a career after university. I did know that I wasn't interested in a career in Chemistry, even though everyone expected me to study that as a degree. I had to be persuaded to return to school to sit the Oxford Entrance Exam. I was told that it didn't matter if I didn't go on to have a career in Chemistry; the important thing was to study for a degree.

In the end, I did well enough in the entrance exams to be awarded an Exhibition (a type of Scholarship) to read Chemistry at Oxford.

During the nine months before starting at Oxford, I had initially hoped to go to Greece to be an au pair, but the opportunity disappeared and so instead I opted to go for a secretarial training. At that point, my life started to unravel. All the stress of the previous years caught up with me. I was doing well on the secretarial course, and even came top in the weekly shorthand test, but I was sleeping poorly and became anxious and depressed. This was the first time that I was given a prescription for anti-depressants.

I can't remember how I felt about giving up the course, but Mum and Dad were kind and invited me to join them in June on a fabulous holiday to Canada. I spent two weeks travelling with them, visiting relatives and then a further week on my own. We didn't talk about my depression; it all got swept under the carpet. It was such a taboo subject, I had no one to talk to about it, and my father didn't want me to get labelled as "emotional".

I did find a medical book in my father's study about anxiety. I tried to read it but can't remember learning anything useful to me. It was a medical textbook.

At the age of 18, I was starting to realise that maybe Mum and Dad didn't know how to support us emotionally. I had always felt loved but not supported emotionally. It was very confusing at the time. Both my parents had been separated from their parents at a critical age and had had to learn to be completely self-reliant and not ask for help. Neither of them had had a role model of a supportive parent to follow. What is interesting to me is that during all this time I continued to try and look after my younger sisters and brother, often listening to their woes, comforting them and lending them money when needed. Many years later, my therapist was to observe that I had become the parent of my siblings in the absence of emotional support from my parents.

At the beginning of my second year at Oxford, I started to feel the pressure. It seemed like I needed to work 24 hours a day to keep up, and it still wouldn't be enough. I was living in the college annexe in a room on the ground floor with an all-glass bay window that jutted out. Unfortunately, there was a leak in the guttering above, and the water dripping on the glass window was so noisy that it felt like Chinese water torture to me. I tried talking to the college bursar to get it fixed, but there was a delay.

I didn't want to admit that I might have any mental health issues, so I concentrated on the leak. Eventually, I cracked and went home to Dorset for the week. During that time, I saw my doctor (who was one of my Dad's partners). I can still remember saying to him "I'm going back to Oxford even if it kills me". I was aware that my doctor seemed very concerned when I said this, and he stressed that my parents were wealthy enough to look after me my whole life if necessary. I can only presume that he was worried I might contemplate taking my own life. At some point, someone prescribed me some diazepam for anxiety and some anti-depressants as well.

I returned to Oxford. At college, we all had a tutor who looked after our emotional wellbeing; it was supposed to be someone who didn't teach us. Unfortunately, in my case, it was one of my Chemistry tutors. I never spoke to him about how I was feeling, but my parents did. My college tutor didn't understand why I hadn't contacted the university counsellors, and he also told my parents that my boyfriend was a bad influence on me. Since my boyfriend had been encouraging me to stay, I was pretty annoyed about this; and it never occurred to me to go and talk to the university counsellors. I can only presume that I was too ashamed to even think about going.

I found that the anti-depressants made me very drowsy and dead in the mornings. When my prescription ran out, I asked my doctor in Oxford if I still needed to take it. My doctor said no. A week later, I wanted it back, but my doctor refused. Later in life, I was very grateful to that doctor; she probably saved me from getting hooked on Lithium. At some point, I realised that I couldn't carry on, but I still couldn't admit to myself that I was only at Oxford because I wanted to please my Dad. Instead, I took the rest of the year off and planned to return the following October to start the second year again.

My parents were lovely, but we still didn't talk about my emotions or mental health. Instead, they suggested that I might like to do a three-month Cordon Bleu cookery course in London. My Mum had done one before she got married. It was good to have a complete break, and I enjoyed the course immensely. By the time September arrived, I knew that I needed to start studying again in time for the beginning of the term in October. It took me only three days to realise that I didn't want to go back. At this point, I was probably starting to realise that my Dad's expectations were based on his unfulfilled hopes and dreams.

I phoned Mum and Dad to give them the news. It was unfortunate that they were due to be going on holiday in three days. My Dad couldn't understand how I could be so good at a subject and not enjoy it. To this day I can't remember exactly what he said to me, but I do remember that my Mum made him phone the next day to apologise to me.

My parents helped me get a place on a Foundation Course in Accountancy. I can't remember exactly why I chose Accountancy. It was another profession which would appease Dad, and it would also allow me to become financially independent of him.

I started work in the autumn of 1981. After about a year, one of the other trainees told me that before I had started work there, someone had seen a letter on file which mentioned something about my depression at Oxford. They had all wondered whether I was going to be a bit of a "nutcase".

After my first set of professional exams PE1, I changed jobs. It was a stressful time. I had three interviews, two with large firms and one with a large, medium-sized firm. One of the large firms didn't offer me a job. The interviewer had asked me about the time I left Oxford. I just said that I had been ill at the time and realised that Chemistry wasn't for me. The interviewer then asked if I had ever been ill like that again, and I said no. I don't know if they deduced that I had had a nervous breakdown or not. It still wasn't something that I talked about.

I liked the large firm, but we had a lot of overtime which ate into my study time. In the first six months I clocked up six weeks of overtime, so when it came for my PE2, I was stressed that perhaps I hadn't done enough work. This gave me anxiety, and it became a vicious cycle. There were five, 3-hour exams in total, to be sat in 2 days.

It was the first time I had ever failed an exam. I went on to fail my PE2 five times in total (every six months) while working for this firm. After that first time I was funding it myself, the 6-week revision course and unpaid leave. Each time I failed, the anxiety got worse. It even started to affect my health, and I started to get tonsillitis several times a year. It was so bad that at one point, my doctor thought I had glandular fever. Eventually, I was to have my tonsils removed.

I changed jobs, and over the next two years, I re-sat my PE2s another four times (making nine times in total in five years). Each time my anxiety got worse, and for at least one set of exams, my doctor prescribed me beta-blockers. I had a meeting with an Occupational Psychologist at work. Even though he mentioned to one of the partners that he wondered if I wanted to pass my exams, I was still offered some external counselling to the total value of £500. The partner was very dismissive of the idea that I didn't want to pass the exams, and I was too. I knew I wanted to pass the exams, but a few years later, I was to wonder if I did want to be an accountant.

I only had one counselling session, and it didn't seem to be of any use. As it was my last attempt at the exams, I did a brain dump; telling the counsellor everything that I could think of that might be making me so anxious in the exams. I don't know what type of counsellor he was, but most of the session, he just listened to me. He only made a couple of comments. The first was to suggest that I apply to postpone my exams by a year, but I already knew that was not possible. The second was more interesting. He said that I had sounded angry when I mentioned that my mother had once said: "perhaps we should have all gone for family therapy". I was a bit stunned at the time and didn't know what to say. When I got home, I realised why I had been angry. My mother knew that there was no way that my father would have ever admitted to any of us needing therapy, let alone go for a family therapy session.

A friend who, I had met on one of my accountancy revision courses, suggested that I might benefit from attending an experiential, personal growth/development workshop with an organisation called Insight Seminars. I had several huge realisations from the workshop "The Awakening Heart Seminar". There were lots of people out there who were as anxious as me about life, and also had difficulties with their families. We did all sorts of healing exercises relating to the relationship with our parents.

I also became aware of how much my emotions were running my life and made a life-changing decision not to have children. I didn't want my emotional insecurities to affect any children. I already knew, from my experiences with my own parents, how much a parent can influence the emotions of their children, and there was no way that I wanted to pass on any of my emotional insecurities to a child. I know that things must have shifted significantly with my Dad. The day after the workshop, I phoned him up just to say that I loved him.

Insight 1 was a very transformative experience for me, but I didn't pass my accountancy exams. I went on to do several workshops with insight and looked at all sorts of things in my life that might have been holding me back as well as creating a vision for my future life.

Insight 2 "The Opening Heart" was another eventful experience. I realised that a lot of the men in my life found it difficult to express their emotions. This included my Dad, one of my best friends who was like a younger brother, and my first boyfriend. After the workshop, I started reading lots of books about loving relationships. There were exercises to do using affirmations, and I can still remember sobbing into my pillow like a baby while saying out loud "Daddy loves me".

One of the workshops was a "Leadership" course. During this course, we set five goals for ourselves: mine included, changing job/career, giving up smoking, finding a loving partner and getting married. As part of the goal-setting process, I realised that I had been so focussed on my career and proving myself to my Dad, that having a loving relationship in my life had fallen to the bottom of my priorities. So now I made this my top priority.

One of the many things I learnt from insight, was a simple formula to help you achieve your goals: be around people who already have it; give it away; and ask for it. We also created a treasure map for our goals – a collage of images that symbolised our goals. Later I made individual collages for each of my goals. (I still use symbols and collages in my life today.)

It was a magical time and a period of enormous transformation for me. I still smile when I look back on everything that I did to find the relationship of my dreams. One of my new friends from insight became engaged in the autumn, and I even went and tried on wedding dresses with her. When the shop assistant asked me when I was getting married, I replied that I wasn't sure, probably next Easter. I didn't even have a boyfriend at the time.

Later that autumn, I got a new job working for a Lloyd's Underwriting Agency as a Syndicate Accountant, and in the spring of 1989, I met my future husband, Mark. We were introduced by my friend who I went with to try on the wedding dresses. We got married in 1990. I did manage to give up smoking eventually, but not until 1996 after several NLP courses.

Insight Seminars was just the start of my personal growth or mental health journey. I started reading all sorts of books about personal development and consciousness. I also had a secret dream; I wanted to change my career and develop something similar to insight, but for the business world. Over the next few years, I became a bit of a self-improvement junkie and went on several courses.

I'd heard about NLP (Neuro-Linguistic Programming) while on the Insight Courses. As a result, I'd started reading about NLP, but eventually, I realised that i needed to understand what I was reading, I needed to go on a course and experience NLP for myself. My husband encouraged me, and I booked up a 3-day course in May 1993, "Exploring your personal mission with NLP", as well as three weeks in July on a summer school "NLP Practitioner Training" both with Julian Russell of Pace Personal Development. This was the real beginning of my mental health healing journey.

NLP is the study of the underlying structure of human experience and communication – how we create our unique mental models of the world and our perception of reality. It can help us to understand how we create and store our memories and also imagine scenarios in the future. It offers tools to help transform those thinking patterns to be more successful and effective in life. It was discovered or created by Richard Bandler and John Grinder when they modelled three excellent therapists and resulted in NLP modelling tools to model any field of human excellence.

I found NLP not only fascinating but very transformative. I started to heal hurtful memories, improve my communication skills, develop greater emotional resilience and find new ways to set and achieve goals that worked. I booked up to do my Master Practitioner in NLP, 21 days, in 3-day modules, starting in September. During this course, I also discovered that I was very good at picking up other peoples' feelings. When I had been feeling so anxious at work, I now realised I had been picking up on my boss's anxiety that had that fed into my own anxiety. It was a vicious circle. But I still didn't want to admit, even to myself, that I had any mental health problems. This discovery was just the beginning of my journey to improve my boundaries, to separate out my feelings from other people's needs and stick up for myself.

Some years later, I attended another Robert Dilts NLP workshop "Identity & Evolutionary Change". This was significant in two ways. Firstly, I was starting to realise that this was an area that was particularly meaningful for me. Parental expectations, particularly my father's, had had a significant impact on my life, and I was learning to break free and discover who I wanted to be. Secondly, there was a very interesting identity change process during the workshop using Carol Pearson's six archetypes of transformation from her book "The Hero Within". What was fascinating to me was that, as Robert described the six archetypes, I became convinced that I had read the book, and when I got home, I discovered the book on my bookshelf. I had bought and read it six years earlier, but at that time had not understood how to apply it to my life.

The summer of 1999 I flew to California to attend two four-week NLP trainings at NLPU (NLP University): Advanced NLP Modelling & Research training with Robert Dilts, Judy DeLozier and David Gordon; and NLP Trainer Training with Robert & Judy. All three of them are excellent NLP modellers and were part of the original team working with the creators of NLP, Richard Bandler and

John Grinder. They are continually developing new NLP theories, models and processes, and to this day, the modelling workshop was the best NLP course I have ever been on. Once I had returned home, it gave me the skills to develop my own materials.

All the learnings during my two months in California were going to take a while to integrate, and I continued to take several advanced NLP trainings over the next year.

I also purchased some book about Joseph Campbell, books, videos and the whole idea of the Hero's Journey very inspiring. He was always encouraging people to follow their bliss and be true to themselves. This was particularly important to me as I went on my own journey to break free from my parents' expectations, to create my own path in life and become authentic. The Hero's Journey itself is a metaphor for a transformation of consciousness, a journey of awakening and discovery as we travel through life and navigate the ups and downs of life.

My interest in symbols, and their psychological and spiritual significance, was growing. The next year was very intense, a period of immense learning, growth and transformation culminating in creating my own series of workshops, The Alchemy and Artistry of NLP, based on NLP combined with the Hero's Journey.

It was an exciting time, and everything was moving quickly. I created my own NLP model called "Living Life as a Heroic Adventure". It was based on a modelling project I did looking at three people who inspired me (Joseph Campbell, Richard Feynman and Vusamazulu Credo Mutwa); to be authentic, speak the truth, follow my own path, and create meaning and purpose in my own life. I used this as the basis to promote my first solo NLP workshop, which I ran in February 2002 "Crossing the Threshold Following the Path of the Hero's Journey".

I was living my dream, and as Joseph Campbell called it "following my bliss" and helping others to do the same. My workshop series totalled 22 days, and I ran it all the way through two years in a row between Sept and April in 2002/3 and 2003/4.

I created the brochure in the Easter of 2002 in time to launch it at the Mind Body Spirit Festival in May. The third workshop in the series combined NLP modelling with Carol Pearson's Archetypes of Transformation and was designed as a journey of discovery, spiritual awakening and evolution of consciousness. A month after I created the brochure, I received an invitation from Carol to attend her first workshop outside of the USA, in the UK. It was yet another serendipity on my journey. Eventually, when I came to run my own workshop, I created an NLP modelling process to help the participants model their archetypal strengths and unique gifts.

I was also offering coaching journeys using the same principles: helping others to find and follow their bliss, be authentic and speak their truth, follow their own path or "hero's journey"; develop their unique gifts and talents; manifest their creative potential and turn their dreams into reality.

I continued with my one-to-one coaching journeys until about 2008/9. I had a couple of clients who were trained in Carol Pearson's archetypes, and it was a joy to continue to develop new processes combining NLP and archetypes.

I have been aware for a long time of the connection between physical and mental health, but it took a long time for me to realise that I had a very unhelpful belief that had a negative impact on my physical health. It also didn't help that I had been brought up with the thought that psychosomatic illnesses were not real illnesses and were dismissed as "all in the mind" as if they were not real.

I had started to explore the health applications of NLP in 2008, when I attended Robert Fletcher's talk at the NLP conference. Robert had created a body of knowledge called Thought Pattern Management (TPM) combining health, hypnosis, accelerated learning and NLP. I was his demonstration subject at the conference, and in 2009 I attended his three-week TPM training. I particularly explored how I could use his techniques to help heal my inner child and my early childhood memories.

In 2015 and 2016 I had a few health setbacks that knocked my emotional resilience once more, and I found myself thinking that there was no point to life and even thought that perhaps my husband Mark would be better off without me. Luckily, I knew that I would never do anything about it - a long time ago Mark had told me that when the time came, he wanted to die before me because he wouldn't want to live without me. When I realised that I was beginning to focus on everything negative, I knew I needed to do something about it, and this time I had a whole toolkit of inner resources to help me.

I started to look for glimmers of hope and spend more time in nature, paying attention to beauty wherever I found it. I made new friends who shared my interests in art, spirituality and psychology and invited them (individually) to spend the day with me at Kew Gardens. It's a wonderful gift to be able to spend time with a person in nature and get to know them. I was looking for kindred spirits who shared my interests and values.

I had always hoped to run my workshops again one day and to do that I thought that I would need to be in London, but in 2017 something happened that made me re-evaluate my life and where we would be living. In 2014 we had moved out of our house for eight months during a major house renovation. I had always hoped we would be able to stay in London for another ten years, but I knew that Mark wanted to move earlier. Our house had increased in value, and it was our pension fund. In the summer of 2017, just before a trip to Ireland for a wedding in Galway, one of Mark's clients insisted that he do some work before we went. It was his biggest client, and they were notorious for asking Mark to do things at the last minute with no planning. It was the straw that broke the camel's back for Mark, and I realised that up until that moment, I had had no idea of how stressful he found his job. I felt selfish for wanting to stay in London and immediately embraced the idea of moving. A couple of days later Mark came into my office where I was sitting at my computer and said to me "wherever you are is home, and I want it to be a positive move towards something for both of us". I was very moved by this, and it confirmed to me that I had made the right decision.

In September 2019, Mark and I finally made our move to the country. We found our ideal home in Headcorn in Kent, where my brother, who lives with us, can still commute to work. I have been talking to a friend Michelle Hazel, who was a teacher and is now training to be an art therapist, about collaborating with her on my Alchemy & Artistry of NLP workshop series. In October I introduced her to Jenny and Stuart Rayner. We hope to relaunch my workshops for the Lucy Rayner Foundation. It has been an exciting time, and with my 60th birthday in February and our 30th wedding anniversary in

June, it feels like the beginning of a new phase in my life. Jenny and I both have our have our birthdays in February, and we celebrated them together when they came to Kent for a weekend that month.

As I finish writing this, we are in the middle of the Corona Virus shut down, and I realise that mental health awareness has become even more important for the community at large. It has taken me many years to break free from my father's fear of me being labelled as emotional and talk about my own mental health journey. I encourage you all to break the silence, share your personal stories and help to remove the shame and stigma that surround mental health issues. As I was reminded last year on one of the Can Anyone Hear Me conferences "we all have mental health".

I include below some activities that have helped me and my mental health along my journey:

1. Always keep breathing and learn how to use your breath to slow down and quieten the chatter in your mind. I struggled to find a meditation practice that I could keep to, so I bought some mediation and relaxation CDs instead.
2. Make sure you get enough sleep; I have several relaxing sleep CDs that I use when I'm finding it hard to sleep.
3. Pay attention to your inner dialogue. Retrain your inner chatter to be supportive and caring. Changing both the voice tone and the message can transform your life. There are many NLP processes that can help with this. One of my favourite NLP books is "NLP: the new technology of achievement" by Steve Andreas, Charles Faulkner and The NLP Comprehensive Training Team.

4. If you notice you are focussing on everything negative, then start to hunt for what I call "glimmers of hope". Keep a gratitude journal. At one point in my life, I began collecting quotes about hope and overcoming despair and shared them with my online friends. For my Alchemy & Artistry workshops, I created a process I call the "Silver Lining Journal" designed to turn your victim story into a heroic adventure. The stories we tell ourselves are very powerful, and it can be helpful to remember we can shape our lives by the stories we tell ourselves. An important thing to remember is that "the seeds of your greatest gifts are sown on your road of trials".
5. Recognise when you need help and find a trusted friend or counsellor to confide in. I have had two periods in my life when I went to see a therapist regularly once for several months, and the other was for several years. It was so taboo in our family to talk about mental health issues that the first time I cried before I phoned a friend to get a recommendation for a therapist.
6. Remember that life is messy, and we can't control it. It's more about how we respond to it than what happens; it's about learning to dance in the rain. As Joseph Campbell once said, "the Buddhists believe that all life is sorrowful, so then life aims to participate in the sorrows of the world joyfully". I also find it helpful to remember that bullies, and other mean or unpleasant people, are usually more scared than me, and I try not to take the things they say personally.

7. If you need to cry, then let yourself cry fully. There is healing in tears. You only have to watch a child bounce back after crying his or her heart out. It's very therapeutic, go for it. If you find it hard to express your emotions, find a song to listen to that will help you reconnect. After my Dad died (unexpectedly at the age of 62), I was so busy looking after everyone else that I didn't make time for my own grieving process. Eventually late one night I put the headphones on and listened to one of Celine Dion's albums, "Falling Into You", over and over with tears streaming down my face. The album was about broken love affairs, but the emotions were the same and helped me to feel and process my grief for my father. And as I write this, I'm remembering doing the same when I was eighteen and nineteen when I was severely depressed, and I listened to the Super Tramp song "The Logical Song". The words were very powerful for me at the time and helped me to realise that I needed to find out who I was and wanted to become.
8. Try to be authentic and speak your truth wherever possible, but first, make sure you are in an environment that will be supportive.
9. Find a way to bless yourself and others. Catch someone doing something well and tell them about it; be specific. Use mirror work to practice self-love: look at yourself in the mirror, pay attention to your eyes, tell yourself "I love you".
10. Read an inspiring book. One of my all-time favourites is "Man's Search for Meaning: The classic tribute to hope from the Holocaust" by Viktor E Frankl. The description from Amazon

reads "A prominent Viennese psychiatrist before the war, Viktor Frankl was uniquely able to observe the way that both he and others in Auschwitz coped (or didn't) with the experience. He noticed that it was the men who comforted others and who gave away their last piece of bread who survived the longest - and who offered proof that everything can be taken away from us except the ability to choose our attitude in any given set of circumstances. The sort of person the concentration camp prisoner became was the result of an inner decision and not of camp influences alone. Frankl came to believe man's deepest desire is to search for meaning and purpose. This outstanding work offers us all a way to transcend suffering and find significance in the art of living."

11. Read a story about someone who has turned tragedy into hope. Christina Noble's books "Bridge Across My Sorrows" and "Mama Tina" are very inspiring. Christina overcame many tragedies and difficulties in her life to go on to found a worldwide charitable foundation for vulnerable children "The Christina Noble's Children's Foundation" (https://www.cncf.org/).
12. Findsomewheretovolunteerorgivebacktothecommunity– something that you enjoy doing and gives you a sense of purpose. Since 2012, even though I have had a combination of medical conditions that have made it difficult to work, I have been involved in building and supporting several online communities in Facebook in the areas of health, creativity, spirituality and business. I love to support people in following their dreams as well as building supportive communities. It's in my DNA. I hope you can find something that is meaningful for you.

13. Grow something, even if it's just a cutting on your windowsill. There's nothing like getting your hands into some compost and seeing something that you planted growing. I love to collect seeds and take cuttings and then grow "free" plants for my garden. It's wonderful to be able to share them with neighbours and friends. Jade plants (Crassula Ovata) are very easy to grow and to take cuttings. I discovered that if a piece breaks off if you put it in a glass of water, it will develop a root. If a leaf breaks of it will even put roots out into the compost. Today I have one large plant which, flowered last week, and about ten cuttings of various sizes in pots or glasses.
14. Create a mindfulness garden. We recently moved from London to Headcorn in Kent. Now we have the space, I am planning a mandala herb garden and a wildflower labyrinth.
15. Getoutintonaturewheneveryoucan.WhenIlivedinLondon, I loved to go to places like Kew Gardens, the Chelsea Physic Garden and Chiswick House. Now we are in Kent I am loving using my National Trust membership to visit places like Sissinghurst and Scotney Castle.
16. Trainyoureyestolookforbeautywhereveryouare, especially in unexpected places - in the shadows as well as the sunshine. I have found photography a fabulous way to train my eyes. I started taking pictures of beautiful sunsets when I was on holiday and found that I enjoyed it so much that I bought a better camera. I particularly enjoy taking photos with reflections in the lakes.
17. Spend time near water- the sea or lakes or rivers. Research has shown that the negative ions in the air can have a positive effect on depression.

18. Take a walk in a forest. Notice the way the sunshine filters through the leaves and branches. There's something about the smell of composting leaves, moss and trees. All you need to do is type "the smell of the forest or woods" into google, and you will find lots of articles describing the benefits. (https://finlandnaturally.com/experiences/nature/finnish-forest/can-you-believe-this-is-how-15-minutes-in-a-forest-affects-you/)
19. Take up a hobby or a creative pursuit; don't worry about the result or final product, just enjoy the fun of exploring the creative process. If you think you can't paint, collect images that you love and create a collage or a mandala. If it still frightens you, buy a colouring/mandala book. Research has shown creating art and writing poetry is good for your mental health. I love to create mandalas and collages and paint my favourite symbols, and it's a good way to make friends with your unconscious mind.
20. Start a daily practice. Keep a journal. Explore different ways you can use a journal to: understand your dreams; heal your inner child; use positive affirmations; awaken your inner mother; transform your inner dialogue; transform negative habits and create positive ones; and heal the past by writing a new story. I have used a journal many times in my life. I found it particularly helpful when my inner child needed support to create a dialogue between my inner mother and child. The best books on dream interpretation that I have found are: "Inner Work: Using Dreams & Active Imagination for Personal Growth" by Robert A. Johnson: "Dreaming Realities: A Spiritual System to Create Inner Alignment Through Dreams" by Julie Silverthorn & John

Overdurf: and "Dreamwork: using your dreams as the way to self-discovery and personal development" by Maggie Peters. One of the best ways to follow Joseph's Campbell's advice of "follow your bliss" is to keep a dream diary on a regular basis.

21. Explore your beliefs and values. I woke up when I was about 27 years old to realise that I had no idea what was important to me. It took a long time to let go of parental expectations and discover my own values. I also transformed several negative beliefs:
    - "I'm the only one who feels like this" Everyone has ups and downs
    - "It's all my fault" Everyone makes the occasional mistake
22. Learn to pay attention to your body and listen to your inner wisdom and intuition. Are you following your own path, or someone else's or society's expectations? It took me a long time to do this; my body knew a long time before my mind and would manifest as anxiety in my lower abdomen if I was ignoring it.
23. Explore what gives meaning and purpose to your life and perhaps even helps connect you to your spiritual nature. As I spent so long not knowing what was important to me, my first step was to make friends with my unconscious mind. The unconscious speaks in symbols and dreams. Personally, I have used a combination of NLP, creative processes (art, collages, symbols & mandalas, storytelling), archetypal psychology, and mythology and the Hero's Journey to make friends with my unconscious.

24. Remember that "the seeds of your great gifts are sown on your road to trials". You are unique, and there is only one of you, with your history and gifts. Share your story, and you never know who it will help.

PROFESSIONALS

Maria Steer

B.A.C.P Accredited
Senior Specialist Counsellor and Supervisor.

My name is Maria Steer, and I am an Integrative Humanistic Therapist. I am a BACP (*British Association of Counselling and Psychotherapy*) Accredited Senior Specialist Counsellor and Supervisor. My training is in Gestalt, person-centred, Transactional Analysis and Psychosynthesis. I have also trained in CBT (Cognitive Behavioural Therapy, DBT (Dialectical Behaviour Therapy), Trauma, Sexual Abuse and Personality Disorders, to name a few.

I left school, age 15 years old with no qualifications. I always found school difficult and would be the 'class clown', which would get me excluded. I am now aware that this behaviour took me away from my feelings of fear and humiliation, anyway I digress!

When I was 30 years old, I decided to go back to college and get my qualifications. I had to choose three subjects, and one of them was Psychology. I became hooked! I found it fascinating, and from there started my journey to be a Counsellor. In college, they ran a dyslexia test and it was discovered that I was dyslexic. At last, it made sense as to why I had struggled so much at school.

I qualified as a Counsellor in 1998 and volunteered for the Young Women's project - working with Domestic Abuse and Sexual Abuse victims. In 2001 I started my NHS career in Primary Care Psychology Service.

I have worked in the NHS mental health psychology service, for over 19 years, which I love. During this time, I have worked in many different locations, which have sometimes been challenging but also rewarding. As well as working within the NHS, I also have a private practice which gives me the opportunity and flexibility to work longer with clients.

A question I am asked a lot is "What is a humanistic integrative therapist"? I explain it, as exploring your past, present and future - this makes me sound like a fortune teller! Which considering I come from a Romany Gypsy background, makes me smile.

I work with the whole person - mind, body, and spirit and believe the therapeutic relationship is the most important aspect, in the way I work. I suppose you could say I tailor the therapy to the individual, as no single approach works for everyone. I believe each person is unique and therefore, so is their therapeutic process.

I am honored to contribute to 'LET YOUR TRUTHS Set You Free'. I am passionate about how people can manage and overcome mental health issues, which may impact on their relationships and everyday living, therefore not allowing them to reach their true potential.

This book can help in showing the reader that there is support and help out there and that they are not alone in this.

I noticed these individual stories were able to show that mental health can present itself in many ways. The thread that ran through all these narratives for me was that of loss. This can have many faces job's, loved ones, friendship's, relationship's, as well as the loss of self - the list can go on. Anxiety, self-esteem, confidence and depression, were some of the presentations that were being described throughout these stories. It was also voiced that having someone to talk things through with, even though they may be difficult – helped. As well as finding the right therapist, where you can safely explore the pain you are experiencing and find your way of working through it.

"Although the world is full of suffering,
it is full also of the overcoming of it"

Helen Keller

Paula Wynter

Consultant Child and Educational Psychologist

Each story takes the reader on a journey transcending years of brokenness, heartache and trauma to a place of greater understanding about themselves and ultimately peace. For some, happy, innocent lives were suddenly crushed, catapulting them into an endless spiral of sadness; no sense of joy; one negative event after the next. For others', they never felt like they belonged, they were not nurtured or shown love; the natural attachment between a mother and a child was never established, leading to years of feeling unloved, unwanted and being angry at the world.

While each story starts off differently, there are several common themes—one of the most prominent being 'Rejection' and 'Loss'.

Psychologists have found that rejection can damage our need to belong; it can cause aggression and anger and impacts significantly on our sense of self and self-worth. Many of the stories talks about 'not fitting in', 'not belonging', feeling invisible, or even feeling emotionally abandoned; where pain is not recognised, not acknowledged or at times blatantly ignored. Some of the writers expressed that they often felt different, ugly or that they didn't fit in. The need for external validation from friends, partners and family members became their ultimate goal; "being perfect", "going the extra mile" or for some changing their behaviour in order to feel valued or to fit in; but this of course was unsustainable.

Feeling positive emotions is linked to meeting the need to feel loved and respected. Maslow's Hierarchy of Needs theory (established 70 years ago) and psychologists such as Baumeister and Leary who built on Maslow's idea of 'love and belonging' found that feelings of belonging is a fundamental need; feeling isolated or left out can have negative consequences for mental and physical health and this is reflected in these real-life stories.

Loss features across the stories regularly. Loss of self, a childhood, a parent, loss of a relationship or even loss of an identity. For many, reoccurring themes of loss throughout their lives, compounded by rejection; led to many years of feeling out of control and wanting to give up on life.

Several of the stories referenced that they coped with their anguish through self-medicating (using drugs, alcohol) and self-harm. Disassociation was also used as a coping mechanism and refers to a disconnection between a person's thoughts, memories, feelings, and actions and is a way of the brain compartmentalising trauma to help manage pain. This could be emotional or physical pain.

When dissociation occurs, there is a detachment from the situation or the reality, mentally escaping from the fear or pain. This may make it difficult to remember the details of the experience later.

Each story has value and allows the reader to see that change or transition can be destabilising, whether it's a geographical move, a change of school, job or moving from one developmental phase to the next. If the transition doesn't meet a personal expectation or the expectation of others, this can be detrimental to one's mental health.

As the individuals went from one painful event to the other, they inevitably reached a very low point. There was a reoccurring cycle of normality, pain, medical intervention and then a sense of normality again. So many of the real-life stories spoke about wanting to be loved, to belong, to be needed, or accepted. On a good day, there was hope in the midst of their pain, a reason or purpose to continue to march forward, but on a bad day there would be feelings of self-loathing, inadequacy, rejection, shame, anger and complete sadness; which for many led to suicidal thoughts and attempting to take their own life.

The stories often spoke of fear 'the threat of harm, real or imagined'. Fear for some caused emotional paralysis, preventing them from moving on from the pain that for so many years held them in 'captivity'. Some of the stories spoke of running from their reality. For others, fear caused physical paralysis, preventing them from being able to move physically. It just goes to show how much the mind is like a battlefield; without the right 'armour' defeat is inevitable.

Each of these real-life stories, has provided a glimpse into the lives of those who dared to be vulnerable in search of the right 'armour' (person, therapeutic approach or the tools) needed to kick -start their recovery. For many, it took a long time before they were in the right place to heal. For others, they needed to find the right person who would understand them in order to find their inner peace. All the writers discovered that there is 'light in their darkness'. Some went on a quest for self-healing and enlightenment, others found therapeutic interventions, where they were able to establish a rapport with a therapist or counsellor whom they could connect with. These tools enabled them to be in a good place to heal, some, of course, were further along than others, as healing is a process; a journey.

Many of the writers showed great insight into knowing when their mental health was starting to wane. They speak of things becoming darker, their mood changing; perhaps feeling the need to isolate to their bedroom. Whilst some were able to seek medical advice, there didn't appear to be many early intervention resources or services to stop their mental health from spiraling out of control.

In my work, I have encouraged clients to use positive self-talk or to use positive affirmations, i.e. telling yourself "I can do this", "I am a success", "I am beautiful", "I have great potential", writing these positive affirmations out and keeping them close by really can make a difference; sometimes you need a reminder of just how awesome you are.

I also find that positive reframing helps. When people make negative comments about you or you hear yourself saying it; change the sentence into a positive. Instead of saying "I always need help, because I can't do it", you could say "I can do this, but I just need a little bit of help". Journaling your thoughts is a powerful tool, so too is openly forgiving yourself, showing self-compassion, gentleness and expressing gratitude. When I am working with vulnerable people, I remind myself to 'love on purpose'. This involves not only saying you care but showing you care, demonstrating it, giving your time, making the call, patiently waiting for them to have the courage to speak and just listening.

While setting up and running a weekly activity-based mental health project for adults with low-level mental health, I saw first-hand how much the volunteers' commitment was to show kindness. Encouraging connections and to help build relationships was fundamental to the healing process. The project highlighted to its members that it is okay not to feel okay. It provided a safe environment to talk, to ask for help, to highlight the goodness within themselves and most importantly, to encourage them to learn to love themselves.

A BRIEF BIOGRAPHY

Paula Wynter is a highly experienced Consultant Child and Educational Psychologist with over 20 years' experience. She works independently within private practice, conducting comprehensive psychological assessments and clinical interviews.

Since completing her professional training at University College London, Paula has acquired extensive knowledge and experience in assessing children and adults with a diverse range of Special Educational Needs (SEN) including children with profound and Multiple Learning Difficulties (PMLD), Severe Learning Difficulties (SLD), Autism (ASD), Attention Deficit Hyperactivity Disorder (ADHD), rare genetic disorders, brain injury, road traffic accidents etc. She also assesses the behaviour and mental health needs of her clients. Paula continues to work with vulnerable children and adults within the education sector and industry. She provides expert witness reports for the Courts, and she is also a trained mediator in SEN and Family (all issues) matters.

WHY I DECIDED TO CONTRIBUTE TO THE BOOK.

As a psychologist, I am interested to hear about the lives of others. The highs the lows, the early life experiences that have helped shape who we are. Every moment and every experience in life can be used to inform our future, to understand further how best to navigate new and sometimes challenging situations; nothing is wasted.

There is always something to learn by hearing others' personal accounts of the joy, pain and how they overcame adversity. These real-life stories will help others who are suffering from their mental health to know that they are not alone. It provides an invaluable insight into the complexity of mental health. The book is a useful resource that will allow the reader to draw parallels with their own lives and in doing so will enable them to find new ways to heal possibly.

I have learned so much from each and every real-life story, which I can use not only to inform my own practice but to get involved in planning intervention; to bridge the gap in the help available and to champion the need for early intervention.

Melanie Yea

Learning & Wellbeing Specialist,
NLP Master Practitioner (ANLP accredited) Coach and Facilitator.

As a Neuro Linguistic Programming Master Practitioner and Coach and as a person, I am inspired by the bravery of these people telling their stories so that others may know they are not alone and gain strength to move forward.

For that reason, I'm going to start at the very beginning of my journey as a therapist, which was not my original intention for my small part in this book. However, to do anything else would feel inauthentic and detract from the power that I believe can be found in these pages.

I discovered Neuro-Linguistic Programming (NLP) when I was experiencing severe panic attacks and anxiety. I had left my job and had moved in with my parents and desperately needed a way to find relief from the exhausting and almost constant anxiety.

I didn't know at the time that the anxiety was a result of Post-Traumatic Stress Disorder that I had been diagnosed with 14 years previously at the age of 17, 2 years after being raped by a friend in their kitchen. With the PTSD came nightmares, self-harming, panic attacks and agoraphobia.

I didn't know at the time that once your brain gets good at running a particular program, in this case fear, it can get triggered and run it without you consciously choosing too. My unconscious was creating an almost constant state of panic, even though consciously I wanted the exact opposite.

If you have experienced anxiety, you will know that it is physically and mentally draining.

Our thoughts and feelings impact us physically. This is the mind-body connection; we are a circuit. Whatever you have been through emotionally will have impacted you physically too.

My first session of NLP, I couldn't believe how the practitioner knew what I was thinking or how he could guide me as if he was inside my head. I know now that he could see from my eye movements (even though my eyes were closed) and body language that I was visually running something traumatic through my mind. He was able to run the whole session completely content-free, which means I didn't have to tell him anything unless I really wanted to, which I didn't.

After the session, I knew I needed to learn how he had done it, and over the coming years, I trained until I became a Master NLP Practitioner and Trainer. I intended to learn more about my brain and how I could have more control of my thoughts, feelings and behaviour and feel less out of control.

I am very happy to say that I achieved that and while I still have bad day's they are very rare and not all that bad.

Naturally, I realised that I could help other people through one to one NLP coaching sessions and am so grateful that I can. Through understanding how someone is getting their current outcome, I am able to undo that program, and along with the hard work of the client, we put in place a new internal strategy that elicits a better more useful outcome for the client.

Our unconscious mind always has a positive intention for us. With anxiety or phobias, it is looking to protect us from possible danger. Once we take the time to sit down with a good NLP therapist who we feel comfortable with, we can unpick even the deepest thought process, and replace it.

Sometimes one session is enough, and other times a more consistent approach is required to support the person through a gradual change of mindset, towards the reality that they so desperately want. People are often surprised at how swift the changes can be.

There is a common thread through-out the truths told in this book. People feeling out of control and not knowing how to process emotion. Neuro-Linguistic Programming is quite literally the language of the mind. NLP breaks down into very simple terms how we are thinking about things and how that is then making us feel. The knowledge and understanding that NLP gives can give us back control over our state and the tools to recognise and manage our emotions. In my opinion, it should be taught to everyone from a young age, for these very reasons.

We experience the world around us and then decode it internally. By this, I mean, we make sense of things that happen, or we try to. This can be a long and fraught process for those of us who have been through traumatic events, as described by some of the courageous people in this book. We can draw incorrect and destructive conclusions based on these experiences.

To help yourself smooth out this process and draw healthy, empowering conclusions which will then become beliefs and values which will drive you forward towards a brighter more enjoyable future, a good therapist, who you feel comfortable with is key.

I heard a quote a while ago which stayed in my head, and it was "You know you have truly forgiven when you can say thank you, for that experience" This is a powerful quote and you might have a strong reaction to it, and that's okay, I did too. However, the more I have thought on it, the more sense it has made, and as an intention, it is useful because it encourages us to look for the gratitude.

Like most people who go through trauma, I don't want to say that I am the person I am because of it, I want to say that I am the person I am in spite of it. Either way I am incredibly grateful and proud to do the work that I do and to be the person I am and I'm not sure an easier road would have led me here, so "Thank you for that experience"

Who do you want to be? What is your first step towards that? When are you going to take that step?

Dr. Filippo Passetti

MD PhD MRCPsych

The stories in "Let your truths set you free" will resonate with many mental health professionals: these are like the many, ordinary, tragic stories of loss, trauma, abuse, loneliness and fear that they grapple with on a daily basis. It is tempting to dismiss them as just that, ordinary tragedies that one would do well not to stare at for too long, retreating behind the screen of professional detachment. And yet, the same stories are also tremendously significant, for both the teller and the listener.

It is a fact of how our minds work that we are storytellers: we learn, understand and grow through storytelling. Wherever we go, every minute of our day, our minds offer us 'stories' about our circumstances past, present and future. These stories tell us who we are, how life and the world are treating us and whether we will succeed or fail. It is these stories that determine whether we are happy, sad, confident, lonely, frustrated or angry. It was the Greek philosopher Epictetus who first suggested that "men are disturbed not by things, but by the view which they take of them".

We also heal through storytelling. The first time Charley, Chenelle, Claudia and any of the other contributors to this book were able to create a story about their ordeal that had meaning, and they could keep that meaning, that's when they started to heal. Similarly, now that those stories have been written they will invite others to find meaning in their own, sometimes confusing and sometimes tragic experiences. They also help us, mental health professionals, understand what it is that heals people, lifting them from the shadows of their traumas and fears.

One of the great storytellers, Tolstoy, opens his Anna Karenina with the sentence "All happy families are alike, but each unhappy family is unhappy in its own way". That is true. Yet, many of the stories here describe similar trajectories. At the start, there are vulnerabilities, be these a physical illness, learning disability, parental mental illness, loneliness or a history of abuse. Sometimes there is a clear precipitating factor: a loss or a trauma. Almost invariably, there is a then a long gap before the needed source of healing can be accessed. It is during this time that, in a desperate search for meaning and relief from mental pain, the traumas multiply and accumulate through the use of drugs, self-harm, the development of emotional instability, or the reliance on an unhelpful relationship. Could those gaps be shortened? Some of the stories point to difficulties with accessing help, be this formal or informal. Most talk about lack of understanding: by doctors, other professionals, parents, peers. For some of the authors, the realisation of the cost to them of that delay in accessing help is so painful that they have chosen to dedicate their lives (not just write their story), to try and reduce it by fostering understanding.

The last part of the trajectory is the healing. As a mental health professional, I found these parts sometimes quite moving. There is something very powerful about the points in which the authors narratives changed. It is one of the great realisations of Cognitive Behavioural Therapy (CBT, mentioned in several of the stories) and other psychological therapies, that we don't have to 'take' the thoughts (or the 'stories') that our minds offer us: of all the thoughts we can have, all other things being equal (by which I mean, provided they are equally true), we can choose those that are helpful instead of those that are unhelpful.

How does that switch happen? In some of the stories, there is an explicit reference to choice and acceptance ('life is what you make it', says one). In others, there is a medication (e.g. ayahuasca), a long-awaited diagnosis, a discovery of a new, more helpful lifestyle (exercise, mindfulness, martial arts). In almost all, there is the experience of being 'touched' by someone: a counsellor, a life partner, a self-help group participant. All these experiences seem to have exerted the healing effect to stimulate a new sense of self-compassion, a sense that even though life is tough 'you are not alone', that it is ok to talk about your feelings and seek help. This, I think, is the core message that runs through all the stories.

Medications and diagnoses are mentioned in many of the stories. As a psychiatrist, I am well aware of the roles and limitations of diagnosis and medication. Diagnosis can help understand and make predictions about the response to treatment and prognosis. Medication can provide a stable platform on which change can take place. However, just like the healing power of personal interaction, their greatest potential is, again, in eliciting new stories. Sometimes a diagnosis can generate a useful, healing narrative in someone with mental illness, just like medication can sometimes trigger that switch from a narrative of illness to a narrative of recovery. At other times, a diagnostic label can chain someone to a narrative of unchangeable illness, just like medication can stifle a sense of someone's autonomy. In the end, it is only the stories you tell yourself that truly set you free.

Dr. Filippo Passetti, MD PhD MRCPsych

After studying medicine in Florence (Italy), Filippo went to Cambridge to study towards a PhD in Experimental Psychology. He then trained in clinical psychiatry in Cambridge and London, including lectureships at the Royal Free & UCL and at St. George's Medical Schools. He worked as a consultant psychiatrist in addiction in the NHS for five years before starting in private practice. His main academic interests have been in the neuropsychology of addictive disorders. His main clinical interests include psychological resilience and stress-related disorders, particularly in separating parents, women, LGBT and young people. He is a managing partner of Cognacity Wellbeing, where he leads on the development of its addiction services, including its residential gambling treatment service in Manchester. Outside work, in his mid-life Filippo has taken up kitesurfing and anything resembling it (skateboarding, snowboarding and sliding on slippery floors).